FILLING IN THE GAPS

Five Essays on the Labour History of Western Australia

FILLING IN THE GAPS

Five Essays on the Labour History of Western Australia

I.H. vanden Driesen

ATLANTIC
PUBLISHERS & DISTRIBUTORS

Published by
ATLANTIC PUBLISHERS AND DISTRIBUTORS
B-2, Vishal Enclave, Opp. Rajouri Garden, New Delhi-27
Phones : 25413460, 25429987, 25466842

Sales Office
7/22, Ansari Road, Darya Ganj, New Delhi-110 002
Phones : 23273880, 23285873, 23280451
Fax : 91-11-23285873
web : www.atlanticbooks.com
e-mail : info@atlanticbooks.com

ISBN 81-269-0261-2

Typeset at
APD Computer Graphics, Delhi
Printed in India at
Mehra Offset Press, Delhi

To my grandchildren with love

ACKNOWLEDGMENTS

In the Preface to *A Collection of Essays on Immigration Policy and Population in 19th Century Western Australia*, published in 1986, I remarked on the paucity of scholarly research on the economic and social history of the state during that century. This small offering hopes to go some way towards rectifying that shortcoming. My appointment as an Honorary Senior Research Fellow in the School of Economics and Commerce of The University of Western Australia provided me with all the facilities a researcher could wish for and gave me the opportunity to work undisturbed on projects I had put off for some years. I thank the Head of School, Professor Paul Miller, for his readiness to provide the funds required to put my work into print and I am grateful also for the consistent encouragement of my colleagues and the willingness of the support staff to give generously of their time and expertise. In particular, I must thank Lorna Duffy and Xahlia Jeffcote who were always ready to explain the intricacies of my computer and whose labours readied my untidy manuscript for the publisher. Where errors still persist, the responsibility is mine alone.

I.H. vanden Driesen
The University of Western Australia

CONTENTS

Contents

Introduction

Of the five essays included in this volume, two have been published before. The first as a chapter in *A New History of Western Australia* edited by C.T. Stannage in 1981[1] and the second as an article in *Labour History*, the journal of the Australian Labour History Society, in May 1981.[2] The former describes the establishment and growth of the Trade Union movement in Western Australia in the 19th century and the latter analyses the first major strike staged during that period; a strike which most importantly was the first to make use of the principle of industrial arbitration. When these essays were first published, both pieces were well received, judging by the numerous requests for offprints and by their inclusion in reading lists specified by university courses in Political, Economic and Labour History. But the stock of offprints eventually ran out, as did supplies of the *New History* and the *Labour History* journal and students over the past fifteen years or so have had to do with library holdings despite these being heavily marked and at times scarcely legible. Clearly the time has come for a reprint of both essays, now placed side by side in a single Volume.

The third essay, on the Master and Servant laws touches free labour, convict and aboriginal workers, union history and immigration policy. It forms a backdrop to the entire period and binds together labour's experiences in the 19th century. The law's significance has long been recognised, nonetheless it has not received the scholarly attention it deserves. Only one historian has hitherto examined it in any detail,[3] but there are still gaps to be filled and errors to be put right, hence the need for yet another study.

The essay on Mr. Justice Burnside has been included to demonstrate that at a time when there were many prejudices in the drawing up and application of industrial law there were some like Burnside who brought a rare objectivity to their work and whose impact on the history of their times has yet to be adequately measured.

The final essay, which traces the origins and development of the Employer's Liability Act, was difficult to put together. The bill was introduced and assented to in 1894, at which time Western Australia was no longer a British Colony. The diminished control of the Colonial Office which followed, greatly cut down the volume of official correspondence between Perth and Downing Street and so removed a prolific source from which historical evidence could be drawn. The path followed by the Employers' Liability Act had, therefore, to be teased out from Parliamentary proceedings, newspaper reports and personal memoirs.

The focus of all five essays falls mainly on the 19th and early 20th centuries. This is a period in Western Australian history which has been comparatively neglected, with academic scholarship tending instead to concentrate on events which occurred after Federation in 1901. It is hoped that these essays will go some way towards overcoming this shortcoming.

---

1. C.T. Stannage (ed.), *The New History of Western Australia*, chapter 11, University of Western Australia Press, Nedlands, 1981.
2. *Labour History* No. 40, May 1981, pp. 29-48.
3. F.K. Crowley, 'Master and Servant in Western Australia—1829-1851.' *Journal and Proceedings of the Western Australian Historical Society* (Vol. IV, Parts V and VI).

1

The Evolution of the Trade Union Movement in Western Australia

The growth of trade unionism in Western Australia occurred in three readily identifiable stages. Initially, a movement centred on Perth and Fremantle grew up in the coastal districts in the middle 1880s, and for the most part proceeded along orthodox craft lines. A decade later the opening of the goldfields launched a second and quite separate organisational phase in which the broad based, general union came to acquire a dominant influence. Finally, at the turn of the century the two movements converged to create a coordinated unionism which rapidly made its presence felt in Western Australian affairs.

Early Developments

By the end of the third quarter of the nineteenth century socio-economic conditions in the Eastern colonies had produced an well-entrenched trade union movement but in Western Australia the basis for such a development had yet to emerge. The census of 1870 shows an occupational structure with a strong agricultural bias. In a total population of 24,785 there were 9,291 adult males, and of these some 41 per cent depended for their livelihoods upon agriculture and pasture farming. Two-thirds of this number were proprietors of one order or another, and the remainder comprised an agricultural working class which was both limited in size and thinly spread across a generally inaccessible colony.[1] Traditionally, agricultural workers have been difficult to organise, and in Western Australia the obstacles were such that the likelihood of this occurring was even more remote than usual.

Urban agglomerations were few, and with the exception of Perth and Fremantle there was not one town in 1870 with a total permanent population in excess of a thousand persons.[2] There were industries in some centres, together with the rudiments of an industrial working class; for example, there were fifteen mills and manufactories in Perth and four in Fremantle,[3] but the scale of operations was small and master and man were in close enough personal touch for the emergence of strong class antagonisms to be effectively inhibited. If there were some who were disaffected, the state of the law governing employment was sufficient to deter any attempt at organised action. The English Master and Servant Act of 1842 was applicable in the colony, and under its provisions a breach of contract by a servant — including such as might be caused by a strike — carried a penalty of three months imprisonment with hard labour.[4]

In the circumstances early working-class organisations had social and cultural rather than industrial aims. A Working Men's Association, set up in May 1862, sought to 'raise the moral and intellectual tone of the working class,' and a Mechanics' Institute, founded about a decade earlier, had similar broad objectives. The former drew its members from amongst the ex-convicts, while the latter catered exclusively to 'free' craftsmen,[5] a significant difference which makes it apparent that a sense of working-class solidarity had not yet arisen in Western Australia.

The growth of a modern trade union movement followed certain social and economic changes, which occurred in the 1870s. A boom in lead and copper mining around Northampton and the discovery of high quality pastoral land in the north gave Governors Sir William Robinson (1875-77 and 1880-83) and Sir Napier Broome (1883-89) the confidence to invest heavily in railway and telegraph construction between 1877 and 1885. Successive gold strikes in the Kimberleys, the Pilbara, and at Yilgarn, which came immediately after, provided an additional impetus, and spread abroad the conviction that Western Australia had much to offer. A marked increase in immigration was an early result. In the six years 1883 to 1887 population rose by 37 per cent from 32,086 to 43,820. Some of the newcomers were migrants from Europe, but the majority came from the eastern Australian colonies where turbulent industrial conditions and frequent unemployment stood in sharp contract to the promise held out by the west. Many made straight for the north but others took employment with the railways and in the several occupations stimulated by the expanding economy.[6] There were a number of ex-trade unionists amongst them and it was not long before those who settled in Perth and Fremantle sought to introduce coastal workers to the principles of labour organisation. Easterners were the driving force behind attempts made in mid-1883 to establish a Labour League, which aimed at the introduction of the eight-hour day and 'of inducing employers to place labour on a more satisfactory footing.'[7]

These aims were never achieved. General unions like the League, which seek to bring workers from diverse occupations into a single association, seldom succeed as a first step in labour organisation. They presuppose in their membership a bond of sympathy strong enough to overcome particularistic differences, and this sophistication of outlook the Western Australian worker still did not possess. A large part of the labouring population was made up of 'a servile ex-convict group which was relatively quiescent about its predetermined status in the organic society,'[8] and the free labour segment had not developed that broader class consciousness which permitted it to transcend the narrower interests of a particular craft or employment. Popular support for the League was therefore lacking when it was inaugurated in August 1883, and it quickly degenerated into a mere unemployment benefit society.[9]

Given the prevailing social and economic climate, it is apparent that trade unionism could only take root under very special conditions. It would have to be specific and not general in form, directing its appeal to the self-interest of the worker in a particular employment. Those engaged in that employment would have to be free settlers, preferably with some immigrant ex-unionists amongst them. All these conditions were met in 1884. The Amalgamated Carpenters and Joiners Society was set up in Fremantle in February, and a branch was opened in Perth five months later. The Society was itself a branch of the English union of the same name and was founded by members newly arrived from England.[10] It restricted itself to the organisation of workers in a particular craft, and what is more, a craft which had grown through immigration into the largest single body of free artisans in Fremantle and Perth.[11] Its success was immediate, and the Society has passed into history as the first permanent trade union in Western Australia.

Craft organisation, 'free' labour, and the migrant ex-unionist became the props on which the trade union movement rested in its early years. When the operation of the newly completed railroad necessitated the import of drivers and fireman — there being none with the required skills in Western Australia — many of the new employees turned out to be union men, and they were quick to establish a Locomotive Engine Drivers and Firemens Union in 1885. Similarly, when an increase in the circulation of newspapers followed upon the growth in population and led to the import of skilled compositors from England and Ireland, the compositors brought their union convictions with them, and in 1887 formed the W.A. Typographical Society.[12]

Apart from their role in the establishment of the colony's early unions the growing population of migrant free settlers contributed in other ways to the further development of trade unionism. It was their presence which persuaded the colonial government to reconsider the laws governing master and servant and to introduce a number of amendments despite conservative opposition. After 1882 servants who broke their agreements were no longer automatically liable to imprisonment in the first instance, and after 1886 a fine was imposed and imprisonment followed only if the fine was not paid. Both amendments favoured the embryonic trade union movement by reducing the severity of penalties that could be applied to some forms of union action.[13] Again, in June 1886 a radical middle-class group largely made up of migrants from the eastern states resorted to the time-honoured tactic of seeking working-class allies in their campaign to win seats in the Western Australian legislature. To attract working-class votes they inaugurated an Eight Hours Association whose main objective was the reduction of the length of the working day from nine and half hours to eight. Like its predecessor the Labour League, the Association was somewhat ahead of events in that it was looking for general working-class cooperation at a time when such a sentiment was practically non-existent. Consequently it failed to muster sufficient support to back up its demands with a strike. It was able to add to the growth of unionism in the west by persuading the bootmakers to set up a union in 1886, but this was the Association's only success, and it had all but disappeared by the end of 1887.[14]

The economic advance of the colony over this period was accompanied by a rise in the volume of shipping annually cleared through Fremantle. Employment on the wharves rose in proportion and it was not long before this attracted the attention of unionists in the east. In June 1889 a delegation from the Adelaide Lumpers Union came west on a recruiting mission, and on July 4 a local union was officially inaugurated with 136 members.[15] The Fremantle Lumpers Union differed markedly from the trade societies then in existence since it drew its membership from the ranks of unskilled labour and not from the well-established crafts. It represented an organisational move into a hitherto untapped sector of the working class, and its formation was a significant milestone in the development of unionism in Western Australia.

An important characteristic of these early unions was their willingness to operate within the existing socio-economic framework. There was no commitment to socialism, or for that matter to any form of structural change, an attitude that was in keeping with the conservative outlook of the average worker. In the pursuit of their industrial objectives the unions were seldom militant. They preferred to petition and to protest, as the carpenters did when they unsuccessfully asked for a reduction of the working day in 1885,[16] and as the locomotive engineers did, with better results, when they complained of long hours and an attempted wage cut in 1886.[17] The strike was a little used weapon, partly because of the implications it had for the scanty funds of the unions, and partly because the Master and Servant Act, despite the amendment of 1886, was still weighted in favour of the employers. For instance, when the Lumpers objected to the use of non-union labour and went out on strike, a number of union members were successfully charged under the act with having left their employment without notice. This strong reaction intimidated the union, which decided to compromise and allow non-union labour already employed in the docks to remain at work.[18]

In October 1889 the Eight Hours Association became active again. Though still led by politically inspired members of the radical middle class the Association had obviously learned from its past experiences and now widened its objectives to include 'the systematic organisation of the working class in Western Australia.'[19] Along with an open general membership, which included the working class, the Association encouraged workers to organise by trade, and then bring their several unions into the Association. This strategy was supported by the established unions, whose numbers in the meantime had been increased by the founding of a Watchmakers Society, and they were either represented at or sent messages of sympathy to the first meeting of the reconstituted Association. The lumpers in particular appear to have recognised the advantages inherent in the new arrangements and pressed for a prolification of unions and the ultimate setting up of a federated body which would direct the union world. They saw this as an essential prerequisite to the successful enforcement of union demands 'as the disorganised state of the labour market led only to defeat.'[20] The wisdom of this advice appears to have been appreciated by their fellow unionists. Despite the Association's expressed willingness to strike in support of the eight-hour principle, the unions at no time even suggested that such a course should be adopted.

In this its second phase the record of the Eight Hours Association in the industrial field was considerably in advance of its earlier efforts. It was largely responsible for the formation of the Railway and Public Works Employees Union in 1890, after an unsuccessful strike for reduced hours had ended in several workers being penalised under the Master and Servant Act. The union represented the labourers, navvies and mechanics employed on the construction of the Midland Railway and the city water scheme, and the union's formation can be viewed as a decided advance since it extended the principles of organisation to those engaged on public works.[21] In addition, the association was able to negotiate the eight-hour day in the building trade early in 1890, and to stage an impressive demonstration in support of the eight-hour principle in the same year. The demonstration had no immediate success but the publicity it gave to the issues involved may well have been responsible for some employers, public bodies and large contractors conceding the eight-hour day in 1891.[22]

The generalisation of the eight-hour principle, however, was an objective the Association could not attain. It might well have done so if the message of the demonstration had been pushed home with a strike, but this would have thrust on the working class a role it was still ill equipped to perform. The unions were too few and those outside them too immature in a tactical sense to provide the concerted effort needed for success. This weakness is said to have been clearly recognisable and has been described as the main reason why 'the employers as a body would not yield.'[23]

Within two years of the demonstration the eight-hour day had become an accomplished fact in Western Australia, but economic forces and not the efforts of the Association were responsible for this turn of events. Further gold discoveries in the early nineties, and particularly those at Coolgardie in 1892, led to an exodus from the coast which had severe repercussions on the labour market. Labour was so much in demand 'that it was possible for a man to choose his own master, and naturally the employer working the short day was given the preference; so that without further agitation, even without any acknowledgment of victory or defeat, eight hours became recognised during 1892 as the length of the working day.'[24]

The decade of the 1890s was a watershed in Western Australian history. The rate of economic growth, though promising enough ten years earlier, surpassed the expectations of even the most optimistic and converted a colonial backwater into a new El Dorado. The discovery of the rich goldfields in Coolgardie and Kalgoorlie was the vortex around which much of the new activity turned, but of importance too was the extended programme of public works initiated by the Western Australian government. Independence in 1890 gave the administration of Sir John Forrest the opportunity to borrow heavily abroad for developmental purposes, and the extension of the railways, the Fremantle harbour works, and the construction of a host of public buildings in the larger towns, made the West a hive of industry at a time when the rest of Australia was suffering a slump.

A spectacular increase in population was an accompaniment of these changes. Net immigration added nearly 111,500 persons between 1890 and 1899, and total population rose from 48,502 to 170,258 over the same period.[25] The multifarious needs of this greatly expanded community had an immediate impact on the industrial sector. In 1891 the total of 'Mills, Manufactories and Works' in all Western Australia stood at 209; ten years later there were 662 such establishments, each employing at least four persons.[26]

The combined effects of economic expansion and immigrant influx on the trade union world were of a rather unusual order. At first the movement was given new life and, quantitatively speaking, began to assume quite respectable proportions. Then, with further discoveries on the fields, the lure of gold proved too much for a large proportion of the union membership and many societies collapsed or else existed in name alone. In the first phase a number of new unions appeared as immigrant craftsmen either brought their unions with them or encouraged unionism in hitherto unorganised crafts. Between 1891 and 1894 societies were set up by the bricklayers, plasterers and masons, the building labourers, the tobacco twisters, the engineers, the coach builders, the cabinet makers and the saw mill workers.[27] In the early years of this same period, the older unions, convinced that the time had come to create a more effective coordinating body than the Eight Hours Association, took steps to establish a Trades and Labour Council. This was accomplished in October 1891, when the council was inaugurated by representatives from five major unions, the Bricklayers, Carpenters, Builders Labourers, Tobacco Twisters and Typographical Societies.[28] The declared aim of the Council was to widen the scope of unionism, and to achieve this end it was prepared to concern itself with more than merely trade matters. From the Eight Hours Association it had acquired the tradition of political action and when a city by-election took place in January 1892 it offered support to the candidate whose views were closest to its own.[29] But little was achieved on either the political or industrial fronts: on the one, because a large proportion of the working class were without votes, and on the other, because parochial jealousies within the movement led to internal stresses which undermined the authority of the Council. This last was particularly relevant to the future development of the Trades and Labour Council. The Fremantle Lumpers Union, then the largest society in the west, stayed out of the Council because of the local rivalry between Perth, where most unions were centred, and Fremantle. Without the lumpers, the Council was immeasurably weakened, and not surprisingly collapsed in March 1892.[30]

At the end of 1892 a number of unions meeting in Fremantle resurrected the Trades and Labour Council. The choice of venue was a palliative to the lumpers, as was the decision that future meetings be alternately held in Perth and Fremantle, and this conciliatory spirit had the desired effect of bringing the lumpers into the Council. In place of the general objectives of its predecessor, the reformed Council spelt out its aims in a twelve-point programme. It sought an improvement in the legal status of the working man through the introduction of legislation that made master and servant equal parties in the eyes of the law; that introduced the principle of employers' liability; and gave the working man security in the matter of wage payments. It sought an improvement in his political status by demanding that the existing suffrage, based on property qualifications, be replaced by full manhood suffrage; that the residency qualification be reduced from two years to one, and that electoral procedures which permitted plural voting and favoured the thinly populated pastoral districts be revised. It sought an improvement in his economic status by demanding that Chinese and Kanaka labour be denied entry to the colony; that local industry be encouraged in the interests of employment; and that taxation be made more equitable. Finally, it sought an improvement in the working of the trade union system itself by demanding the legalisation of unions, which until then had to be registered as friendly societies, and by urging the official acceptance of the principles of conciliation and arbitration.[31]

Initially, the resuscitated Trades and Labour Council kept alive the link between the middle and working classes which the Eight Hours Association had originated. In fact, W. Falconer and R. Hornby, the president and secretary respectively of the Association, were elected to similar positions on the Council.[32] This link, however, was destined to be short-lived. Within a year the Council had passed under the control of easterners who, being accustomed to working in purely labour organisations, were unsympathetic to the notion of a class alliance. From then on direction of the trade-union movement was firmly centred in the hands of the working class, and the part-time middle-class leader passed from the labour scene.

The new leaders, of whom the most notable were Chitty Baker of the Typographical Society and George Pearce of the Amalgamated Society of Carpenters and Joiners, were unconvinced of the efficacy of the strike weapon.[33] Their attitude no doubt was influenced by the disastrous effects on the working class of unsuccessful strikes in the eastern states in the early nineties, but equally they must have realised that the union movement in Western Australia lacked the depth required for effective industrial action. In 1893 the Trades and Labour Council was made up of only six unions and there was little prospect of any form of aid from the unorganised sections of the working class. Consequently, political action was considered the means most likely to produce results, on the grounds that influence in the legislature could be used to promote the economic well-being of the unionist. A political division of the Trades and Labour Council known as the Progressive Political League was accordingly formed in October 1893, with branches in the major towns. For its programme the League took over the Trades and Labour Council's manifesto but added to it the specifically political demands that parliaments should be triennially elected, and that members of parliament should be paid.[34]

The Legislative Assembly elections of 1894 gave the League an opportunity to put its political arm to the test. The result was a fiasco. In the country areas the League was unable to field a single candidate, either because there were insufficient supporters on the electoral rolls, or because none could afford the expense of standing for election. In the metropolitan districts the situation was much the same but in addition internal dissension deprived Chitty Baker, the sole candidate, of the League's official support, and he lost badly at North Fremantle. In the end the best that the League could do was to support a number of 'approved' liberal candidates, and though some of these were returned it was poor compensation for the setback which the union political movement had suffered.[35]

It was at this point that the gold strikes began to exercise an inhibiting influence on union development. The discoveries in Kalgoorlie in June 1893 and a succession of finds in the two years following led to an exodus from the coastal districts. The skilled and the unskilled, unionist and non-unionist, master and servant, set off for Kalgoorlie to seek their fortunes. Even George Pearce, secretary of the Carpenters Society and a leading light in the Trades and Labour Council, was amongst them. The pace of union activity fell away over the next two years as 'working class collectivism was dissipated by the frantic individualist search for gold,'[36] and even the Trades and Labour Council failed to meet at all in 1895.

Though the gold frenzy weakened trade unionism it did not bring about its complete destruction. A hard core of the larger unions continued to meet when the tide was at its lowest ebb, and so ensured a base on which the movement could be reconstructed. By 1896 the rush had passed its peak, disappointed prospectors were drifting back to the coast, and perhaps most important of all, it was becoming widely recognised that 'the real profit in the gold rush would be secured by the man who sold the work of his hands to the fortune-seekers.'[37]

The resurgence of economic activity on the coast in the last years of the century broadened the foundations of the trade union movement by increasing the number both of individual unions and of those enrolled within them. Boilermakers, bakers, tailors, painters and decorators, bread carters, bookbinders, hairdressers, and hotel and restaurant workers were all unionised before the end of 1897 and it became apparent that the union movement had more than recovered from its setback of a few years previous.[38] In addition, unionisation spread beyond the crafts and the unskilled to sections of the community which had earlier shown no interest in the movement, notably to the teaching profession and the white-collar public service. Schoolteachers, after several abortive efforts, established the State School Teachers Union of Western Australia in 1899, and in the public service a group of postal workers, despite some initial difficulties, organised themselves into the Electric Telegraphic Association of Western Australia in 1900.[39]

This gradual expansion of the ranks of organised labour did not go unnoticed by the government. The premier, Sir John Forrest, for one, early recognised the significance of what was taking place. Being a far-seeing politician he thought it politic to make concessions to a group interest which if not placated would inevitably come to oppose his administration. The result was that through the 1890s a succession of laws which came on to the statute book made concessions of the sort likely to mollify organised labour. In 1892 an amendment to the Master and Servant Act placed employer and employee on a footing of absolute equality, and both parties were thereafter to be dealt with equally in the case of broken contracts. Two years later the liability of employers to make compensation for personal injuries suffered by workmen in their service was extended and regulated, and in 1895 exhaustive provisions for the regulation and inspection of mines and collieries were legalised. The problem of wage default by employers was taken up next, and a Workmen's Lien Act, introduced in 1897 and strengthened through amendment the following year, gave greater security to workmen in obtaining payment of their wages. Finally, the truck system, where workers were paid in kind instead of cash, and which was productive of serious injustices on the goldfields and in the timber industry, was declared illegal by an Act of 1899 which prohibited the payment of wages in goods rather than in money.[40]

By 1900, therefore, the old master and servant system had been replaced by a fairly comprehensive code of more considerate laws, the development of which owed much to the presence of an organised labour movement. It is particularly significant that the legislation covered many of the demands embodied in the Trades and Labour Council's twelve-point programme, *i.e.*, the equality of master and servant, employers' liability, and the security of wage payments. There can be no better index to Forrest's political sagacity or to the fact that the trade union movement had become a securely entrenched and accepted phenomenon on the coast.

The rebirth of unionism was accompanied by a renewed interest in political activity. In October 1896 the Trades and Labour Council re-entered the political arena with the founding of the Political Labour Party, though with a programme which differed considerably from that of its predecessor, the Labour League. Partly, this may have been due to Forrest having already conceded some of the League's demands, but in the main it would seem that the new party was attempting to discount the impression that it was merely an off-shoot of the Trades and Labour Council. Its platform now embraced electoral reform, payment of members, abolition of the stock tax and import duties on necessities, and free secular and compulsory education.[41] These were not issues specific to the trade union movement, and were clearly designed to so broaden the appeal of the party as to attract a more general support than hitherto. With such support there was the likelihood that labour would in the not too distant future be able to seat its representatives in the legislature in its own right instead of playing its traditional role of supporting liberally minded candidates.

Labour's ambitions for a meaningful political identity were shattered at the state elections of 1897. With members of the legislature still unpaid, candidates proved hard to find, and the Political Labour Party ended up with only one official nominee, Charles Oldham, a builder who had once been president of the Trades and Labour Council.[42] Oldham admittedly was returned, but this solitary success fell far short of the party's original expectations. All the same, these events are of some historical significance. They do more than merely mark labour's independent entry into parliament. They reflect also a growing willingness on the part of the leadership to challenge the existing order by assuming a more assertive role on the political front.

A similar attitude is discernible in labour's approach to industrial affairs over the same period. Until 1897 strike action initiated by the unions was extremely rare, and when it was attempted generally proved unsuccessful. The lumpers for example, failed in 1889 to establish a closed shop on the waterfront, and in 1892 foundry workers at Northam were unable to win a 5½ days week.[43] On a few occasions demands were granted before industrial action became necessary. The Typographical Union secured an increase in wages from the Western Australian Press in 1892,[44] and a year later the Trades and Labour Council was able to get an assurance from the government that the practice of sub-letting contracts for the construction of public works would be banned, but these were exceptions rather than the general rule. The only direct confrontation of any significance which involved a successful strike occurred in 1894 when tobacco twisters in Fremantle struck against a proposal to reduce twisting rates on a special line of tobacco. The men stayed out for nearly weeks and ultimately negotiated a satisfactory agreement with their employer.[45] Given that the union movement had been in existence for a full decade, its record in the field of industrial action up to that point could hardly be described as impressive.

It was in 1896, the year in which the Political Labour Party was founded, that a bolder stance in industrial matters became evident. The expansion of the goldmining industry had triggered off a boom in the coastal districts, and a number of unions took advantage of the call on the services of their members to demand an increase in wages. The lumpers, the bootmakers, the furniture trades, the railway workshops and several unions in the building trades, all struck or threatened to do so at some point between 1896 and 1897 in support of their demands.[46] These were conceded without much resistance by their employers, who it appears were anxious to avoid disruptions which would prevent them from making the most of the prevailing prosperity. The readiness with which the concessions were made, however, seems to have created the impression among some sections of the building trade that their original claims had been too modest, so early in 1897 three unions, the Builders' Labourers, the Carpenters and the Plasterers, demanded a further round of increases.

The unions believed that the employers would once again think it in their economic interest to maintain industrial peace by offering immediate concessions. But of a total of forty-one employers, only thirteen behaved as anticipated. The remainder, who between them employed the majority of the unionists, held that it would be dangerous to give way a second time. They rejected the demands outright, organised an Employers Association, and set up a fund with which to import labour from the eastern colonies.

The unions countered by going out on strike on 1st February and the events which followed make it clear that when it came to a major confrontation, labour's new willingness to take a harder line was not matched by an equal advance in its understanding of union tactics, or by a greater sophistication in its general outlook on industrial matters. The unions began by committing the error of calling out only those who were not receiving the suggested wage rate. Since this had been granted by almost a third of the employers, it meant that some union members continued to work while others were out on strike. As a result the impact of the strike on the building sector as a whole was considerably weakened. That in a clash of this order the leaders should have ignored the 'one out, all out' principle is a measure of their poor grasp of tactics, and that some unionists should have worked while their fellows did not, is indicative of a total absence of a sense of class solidarity. In the circumstances it is not surprising that the arrival on 11th February of the strike-breakers recruited in eastern Australia proved sufficient to bring the episode to an end. Fearful of being replaced the strikers drifted back to work and within a matter of days the building workers strike was over.[47]

The resistance shown by a group of employers during the builders' strike was the first manifestation of a rising sentiment that the time had come to contain the growth of organised labour. The next move in that direction came on the waterfront when a temporary recession in 1898-99 brought an increase in unemployment which it was thought would seriously undermine the influence of the Lumpers Union. The employers however, found themselves confronted by a labour movement which had taken to heart the lessons of 1897, and the final result was an industrial clash which in importance and significance outranks all others in the nineteenth century.

On 15 February 1899 the West Australian Steamship Owners Association posted a notice on the wharves which outlined the conditions on which employment was to be available as from 1 March. The notice declared (a) that henceforth there was to be full freedom of contract on the wharves, a stipulation which implied that there was to be no 'closed shop' on the waterfront and no recognition of the Lumpers Union; (b) that rates were to be reduced all round through a cut in payments for ordinary time, overtime, and holiday work; (c) that the current working day of 8 a.m. to 5 p.m. was to be altered to fall between 6 a.m. and 6 p.m., a condition which effectively wrote off three hours of overtime and (d) that full rates were to be paid only for work actually done, time spent travelling to ships anchored away from the jetties being compensated at a lesser rate, even though the ships were usually stationed there to suit the convenience of the shipping agents.[48]

The immediate rejection of these terms by the Lumpers Union precipitated a strike which lasted for over five weeks and was accompanied by a degree of violence never previously experienced in Western Australia. The long duration of the strike was as much a reflection of the remarkable sense of unity which imbued the lumpers as it was of the Association's determination to crush the union. Yet try as they might there was nothing the steamshipowners could do to undermine the lumpers' solidarity. Soon after their original announcement the Association placed a series of advertisements in the daily newspapers calling for applications from those willing to accept the new terms and emphasising that preference would be given to their old employees, provided they registered before a specific date.[49] When not one of their ex-employees responded, the Association substituted overt inducements for covert threats, and offered permanent employment on weekly wages to 'experienced' men.[50] Again, there was no response from the members of the union. The Association then abandoned all attempts to woo back their former employees and concentrated on building up a 'free' labour force, while simultaneously making arrangements for dock labour to be brought in from the eastern colonies.[51]

It was the use of a skeleton force made up of non-union and imported labour which led to the outbreak of violence on the waterfront. On 6th March there was a portent of things to come when work in the docks was brought to a standstill by a large and belligerent crowd.[52] On the sixteenth and seventeenth of the month workers on several ships were attacked while unloading cargo, and on the former occasion between forty and fifty free labourers were hunted off four ships by a mob of three hundred to four hundred men.[53] A number of cases of intimidation and assault, both on the jetty and in the streets of Fremantle were also reported, and in some instances ended in court. These several incidents prompted the government to station a large contingent of policemen on the wharves, and to close off the jetty to the public. This allowed work to proceed, albeit slowly, in the port, but it only worsened the already embittered atmosphere since the union immediately charged the government with taking sides by supporting the Association's use of non-union labour.[54]

The determined efforts of the shippers to work their vessels with non-union labour gradually pushed all disagreement over wages and working conditions into the background, and made freedom of contract and recognition of the union the main issues in the strike. The Trades and Labour Council was soon of the same opinion. Since the matter of union recognition was considered the most fundamental of all trade union issues, the Council unanimously endorsed the strike, and moved that the general public be asked to contribute towards the maintenance of the lumpers.[55]

When the lists were opened, the response was immediate. Subscriptions flowed in from all directions; from the unions, from employees of various establishments in the city, and from petty businessmen, proving without doubt that there was a considerable sympathy for the strikers in the community.[56]

With both sides firm in their determination not to capitulate, the strike dragged on week after week. Work in the port did not come to a halt, but the volume of goods cleared each day dropped well below normal. This created some concern amongst businessmen in Perth and Fremantle and prompted a growing demand that the questions at issue should be solved through arbitration. Eventually, an ad hoc tribunal was set up, on which the Roman Catholic Bishop Gibney represented the employers, the chairman of the Methodist Conference, the Reverend Rowe, represented the employees, and Anglican Bishop Riley acted as chairman.

After intensive negotiations the tribunal was able to bring the strike to an end on 5th April. According to the agreement finally accepted by both parties the steamship companies retained the freedom to employ whom they pleased provided they maintained the union wage in their contracts. Wages were fixed at the levels set down in the Association's announcement, except for coaling, where the old rates were re-introduced.[57] It might seem that the agreement favoured the employers and that the men gained only the old rate for coaling, but such an interpretation of the agreement misses its significance. It must not be forgotten that recognition of the union had become the main issue in the strike. The Association's willingness to go to arbitration implied that such recognition had been conceded, and its willingness to pay free labour the union rate from then on, showed that it accepted the continued existence of the union in the port.

Historically speaking the strike is important for two major reasons. On the one hand, it provided the first example in Western Australian history of the use of arbitration to settle an industrial dispute. The unions had long desired the introduction of compulsory arbitration but had not been able to create much sympathy for the principle. The lumpers' strike proved its efficacy to both government and employer, and paved the way for the passage of an arbitration bill. On the other hand, the conduct of the lumpers and their sympathisers demonstrated a growing maturity on the part of the working class. The refusal of the union membership to succumb to threats or blandishments, and the readiness of employees in other areas of the economy to provide financial aid to the strikers, shows a sense of solidarity that had never been previously witnessed on a similar scale. By the turn of the century it seemed that the coastal trade union movement had reached a point where it was adequately prepared to make a more positive contribution to Western Australian history than hitherto. Subsequent events were to prove that it had indeed arrived on that threshold.

Goldfields Unionism

Trade unionism on the goldfields grew up quite independently of the movement on the coast. The rush to the 'fields which began with the finds in the Kimberleys and Yilgarn reached a peak with the discoveries in Coolgardie and Kalgoorlie and by the middle nineties a quarter of the Western Australian population was resident on the goldfields. Conditions there were at first not conducive to the emergence of a union movement. The early miners were not wage earners in the service of some mining company; rather they were self-employed, petty entrepreneurs, seeking their individual fortunes and prepared in the meantime to endure the most incredible privation. Many were from the eastern colonies and of these a fair proportion must have had previous trade union experience. Yet, once on the 'fields union principles were put aside as all joined in the feverish scramble for gold. As long as alluvial gold was there for the taking there was little change in the general attitude of the fossicker, but when the alluvial ran out, as it did in one area after another as the nineties progressed, the objective conditions required for the birth of trade unionism came into being and a union movement got under way.

The capital requirements of the alluvial miner were limited enough to be dismissed as negligible. A pick-axe, a barrow, a shovel, a dry-blower or cradle, a small stock of provisions, perhaps a tent; little else was needed, and the expense involved was well within the means of the individual prospector. Reaching the veins of gold that lay below the alluvial, however, was an altogether different proposition. The rock-crushers, steam engines, pit props, cages, and other equipment essential to reef-mining called for a money capital which the average fossicker did not possess. Reef-mining consequently became the province of the goldmining company, and as the one form of mining superseded the other, so also did the status of the goldfields worker deteriorate. Yesterday's entrepreneur became today's wage-earner, and with transformation in his status grew increasingly unwilling to accept living and working conditions which he had been prepared to tolerate when he laboured on his own account.[58] It was upon this increasing resentment that the union movement was initially based, and since it had to await the growth of these sentiments a characteristic of goldfields unionism was a discernible time-lag between the first discovery of gold and the emergence of labour organisation in the mining sector. This pattern was first noticeable in Yilgarn where a Miners Union, the earliest on the goldfields, was set up in 1889, three years after the field was discovered. In Coolgardie the lag was a year shorter, the Coolgardie Miners' Association appearing in 1894; and in Kalgoorlie after a similar time lag a number of mining associations appeared in 1896.

The proliferation of mining unions in the middle nineties was so rapid that by the end of 1896 every town of consequence appears to have had its own society. In addition to those already named there were unions at Kanowna, Mount Malcolm, Menzies, Southern Cross, Mount Margaret, Ullaring, Speakman's Find and Day Dawn.[59] Some were branches of the Amalgamated Miners Association of the eastern colonies; others were quite independent organisations, though given the composition of the mining community, there can be little doubt that a fair slice of their members must have had prior union experience in the east.

The development of the mining towns let to the growth of a variety of employments not directly connected with the extraction of gold. Most fell within the traditional province of the craft society, and it was not long before a number of craft unions appeared. In 1895 a branch of the Carpenters and Joiners, the Goldfields Typographical Society, and the Coolgardie Shop Assistants Union were established, and by 1899 the building workers had followed suit. The only significant craft group directly associated with the mines, and one which came to wield a considerable influence in labour affairs, was that representing the mine engine drivers. Unwilling to amalgamate with the mass of unskilled labour, they formed their own union, the Amalgamated Certified Engine Drivers Association, in 1897. Branches were set up in one town after another, and by the turn of the century the Engine Drivers Union was the most powerful and widespread craft union on the goldfields.[60]

In January 1897 several of the newly established mining unions, conscious of the advantages of coordination, met in conference at Coolgardie. Out of their meeting came two decisions which were destined to influence the future course of union history in Western Australian. The conference resolved, first, that the mining unions should amalgamate and set up a federation with an elaborate administrative structure made up of branches, district councils, and a central executive; and secondly, that an 'open door' policy should be pursued with respect to membership, and that henceforth the skilled and unskilled, not merely in the mines but in all forms of employment, should be included in one and the same organisation. The protagonists of these views, notably Hugh de Largie, John Price and Fred Gilbert, were all recent arrivals from the eastern colonies. Their belief in the efficacy of the comprehensive union, as distinguished from the hitherto established craft principle of one union to one trade, was accompanied by an emphasis on union activity in the political field which led the association to accept *in toto* the political programme of the coastal Trades and Labour Council. That the prescription was an eminently successful one is above question. The Australian Workers Association grew so rapidly in numbers and strength that within two years it was by far the most powerful single force in Western Australian labour affairs.[61]

Unionism in general and the Australian Workers Association in particular received a further impetus in 1898 following steps taken by the government to block the development of deep alluvial mining. Hitherto alluvial mining had been confined to surface operations, but in 1897 deep leads were found at Kanowna and on the North-Eastern Coolgardie fields. The working of deep alluvial required the sinking of shafts, but not the use of expensive capital equipment, and so offered the small prospector a new lease of life. As the law then stood, prospectors were permitted to enter company leases and to work alluvial to within 50 feet (15 m) of the reef. There were no legal restrictions on the depth of the working but as alluvial gold had previously been assumed to lie only on the surface the diggings had invariably been shallow. With the discovery of deep alluvial, prospectors claimed the right to sink shafts on company leases, and in some cases began operations. The mining companies were unwilling to concede this right, and through their influence with the government won an amendment to the law which limited alluvial mining to a maximum depth of 10 feet (3 m). This 'ten foot regulation,' as it was called, effectively curtailed the further development of alluvial mining and also 'confirmed large numbers of men in the knowledge that they were likely to remain wage-earners for the remainder of their lives.'[62] The resulting frustration prompted many to take out union membership, more often than not in the Australian Workers Association.

With increasing union activity on the goldfields, employee resistance to adverse working conditions began to stiffen. The building trades in particular were involved in a number of wage disputes, two of which led to strikes in 1898. This made it evident to both craft and general unionist alike that the interests of the goldfields movement demanded a greater degree of coordination. With this objective in view a conference of unions was called in July 1898, and out of its deliberations emerged a Trades and Labour Council with a similar programme and structure to that already established on the coast.[63]

By the last years of the 1890s, then, the twin arms of the union movement in Western Australia had reached a roughly comparable stage of development. The union was well established on both the coast and the goldfields, and in each of these areas a Trades and Labour Council had been set up. On the structural side there were differences in that the craft union played a lesser role in Kalgoorlie that it did in Perth, and the Australian Workers Association did not have a coastal counterpart. But these differences declined in importance when the two movements merged at the turn of the century to lay the foundations of the prevailing system of industrial relations in the western state.

Though it is evident that firmly based union movements existed on the coast and the goldfields by 1900 a paucity of statistical data makes it difficult to estimate the number of unions in existence at any one time. It has been estimated that by 1899 there were thirty unions on the coast and an equal number on the goldfields, but these are only approximate figures since the formation or demise of unions was not always reported.[64] On membership even less can be said. Extant union records are too few to allow a total to be computed and estimates vary so widely that they are of little practical value. Such evidence as there is makes it clear that in many employments a large proportion of the workers were not members of the union, and that in general the organised were heavily outnumbered by those who were not. The influence of the unions however, cannot be assessed by the size of their paid-up memberships. Incidents such as the builders' and lumpers' strikes demonstrated that their impact on society could be far from inconsequential.

A gradual decline in goldmining was a characteristic of the first decade of the twentieth century. Production reached a peak in 1903 and then fell off slowly as the more easily worked deposits were exhausted. The workforce in the industry decreased simultaneously from 20,716 in 1903 to 16,279 in 1910, though employment in the mines still remained one of the most important occupations in the state.[65] Over the same period Western Australia's population continued to grow rapidly, rising from 179,708 in 1900 to 276,832 in 1910, despite a decline in net migration between 1905 and 1909.[66] The threatened imbalance in the labour market was largely overcome by compensatory developments in other areas of the economy. The encouragement of agriculture and rural settlement by the government absorbed many a migrant and ex-miner; a public works policy which embraced a considerable expansion of the railways rapidly made the latter one of the largest employers in the state;[67] and an extension of secondary industry in which the number of industrial establishments rose from 632 in 1900 to 822 in 1910, provided further opportunities for employment.[68] These last two developments did much to assure the continued growth of the trade union movement. Official returns for these years are available in fair detail and show an increase in the number of unions from 56 in 1901 to 166 in 1911. The 1901 figure, though somewhat lower than that posited for 1899, reflects the amalgamation of a few of the smaller unions and not of a weakening in the enthusiasm for unionisation. Membership showed a corresponding increase over the same period, rising from 9,370 in 1901 to 31,288 in

1911. In fact the number enrolled in 1911 must have been well in excess of the given total, since the returns for that year are known to be incomplete.[69] A notable feature of this period of rapid expansion was the decline in the numerical significance of the unions on the goldfields and the rise of those centred in the Perth metropolitan area. In 1901 49.7 per cent of all unionists came from the eastern districts and 41.6 per cent from the southwest; in 1911 the eastern districts accounted for only 27.3 per cent and the southwest for 69 per cent.[70]

The first reliable estimate of union penetration of the total Western Australian workforce was made by the Commonwealth Bureau of Census and Statistics in 1912. By comparing the total number of unionists with the total number of employees aged twenty and above, the bureau concluded that 40.90 per cent of the state's male workers were unionists in 1912. This figure compares favourably with the Commonwealth average of 43.99 per cent for the same year,[71] and when it is borne in mind that unionism was some thirty years older in the eastern states, the comparative rapidity of union penetration in Western Australia becomes apparent.

The initiative in bringing together the two strands of the Western Australian trade union movement was taken by the Australian Workers Association when it convened a Western Australian Trades and Labour Congress in Coolgardie in April 1899. Present at the congress were representatives from the coastal Trades and Labour Council and some of the larger coastal unions, but the largest number of delegates by far were from the goldfields, and of these over half were members of the Australian Workers Association.[72]

The delegates sat down to an agenda which covered practically every facet of working-class activity, and after six days of discussion put their conclusions in a series of resolutions. On the industrial side the most important of these resolutions supported the introduction of a compulsory conciliation and arbitration act similar to that then in force in New Zealand, and of a comprehensive trade union bill which provided for the registration of unions. The one would oblige employers to consider grievances whenever these arose, instead of waiting until they were forced to do so through a confrontation with labour; the other would remove the stigma of illegality which laws inherited from England in 1829 and still unrepealed had conferred on all trade union activities. On the political side much attention was paid to electoral reform, and the more important resolutions called for a redistribution of seats according to population and for the payment of members of parliament. Both issues were of particular importance to the labour movement; the former because it would permit the proper representation of the new mining towns, and the latter because it would free labour representatives from the financial disabilities consequent upon unpaid service in the legislature.[73] In addition, the congress declared its support for Australian federation, and unanimously voted in favour of 'the national ownership of all means of production and distribution, for the benefit of all.'[74] The resolution is of interest since it committed to socialism a trade union movement which until then had not professed a political philosophy, though it was to be a long time before the unionists put forward a specifically socialist programme.

One of the most notable aspects of the congress was its concern for the future organisation of the labour movement. In his inaugural address the president, Hugh de Largie of the A.W.A., stressed the connection between working-class unity and the achievement of industrial reform, and urged the necessity for 'common action in the colony and ... a political programme mapped out and concerted action taken in regard to it.' This amounted to a call for serious political action on the part of the trade union movement, and implied that the congress should pursue on a colony-wide scale what the coastal Political Labour Party had sought to do. The meeting's response was to draw up plans which envisaged the establishment of a Western Australian division of the Australian Labour Federation that would seek direct representation in both state and federal parliaments. The federation was to have two district councils, one on the goldfields and the other on the coast, and a joint parliamentary committee set up by these councils to implement its programme. Wherever possible the federation would field its own candidates but if financial considerations — such as the non-payment of representatives — made this difficult, the federation would support candidates who were prepared to subscribe to a minimum three-point programme which demanded the redistribution of seats according to population, the payment of members of parliament and the introduction of a compulsory arbitration act. To ensure that the proposed Labour Federation was adequately publicised, and that the working class was kept informed of the latest developments on the industrial and political fronts, the congress decided that steps should be taken to launch an independent labour newspaper.[75]

While the congress of 1899 succeeded in laying the foundations for a coordinated trade union movement, its achievements in other directions were of a very limited order. The funding of a labour newspaper presented no problems and in June 1900 the *Westralian Worker* commenced publication with T.H. Bath, an A.W.A. man, as editor.[76] The demand that parliamentary representatives should be paid also had a favourable outcome, but this owed little to the unions' espousal of the principle. A large number of parliamentary members found it in their self-interest to support the innovation, and it became law in December 1900, despite the opposition of Forrest and some of his cabinet.[77] Beyond this, little else was immediately accomplished. The proposals for setting up a branch of the Australian Labour Federation were not implemented, for while the principle of coordinated action was accepted by all, dissension on the goldfields, and fears on the part of the coastal unions that they would be forced into a subordinate role, prevented the scheme from getting under way. Similarly, the resolutions on electoral reform and the legalisation of the trade unions failed to produce satisfactory results. Forrest at first refused even to discuss the issues with union representatives, but later in the year conceded the need for a redistribution of seats and included such a scheme in the Constitution Amendment bill of 1899.[78] The new arrangements, however, failed to remove the anomalies of which the unions complained and the goldfields remained grossly under-represented.

The resolution which called for the introduction of a conciliation and arbitration bill had an altogether frustrating outcome. Forrest had expressed his opposition to arbitration on a number of occasions in the late 1890s and it seemed there was nothing the unions could do to bring him round to their way of thinking.[79] The severity of the lumpers' strike, which occurred while the congress was in session, and the fact that it was settled through voluntary arbitration, led the premier to reverse his stand, and in August 1899 a Compulsory Conciliation and Arbitration Act was brought forward in the Legislative Assembly. Yet when the bill reached the committee stage a small group of parliamentarians who were opposed to its provisions forced one postponement after another, and when the end of the session arrived the bill was still in committee and had to be discharged.[80]

The disappointing results of the first congress coloured the proceedings of the Second Trades and Labour Congress when it met in Perth in August 1900. Fifty-five delegates representing thirty-two labour organisations passed a series of resolutions, ranging from the need for a shops and factories act, to the advantages of setting up mining, technical and agricultural colleges. But two questions dominated all else; how to ensure the passage of a conciliation and arbitration act, and how to secure maximum labour representation at the forthcoming federal and state elections.[81] In sharp contrast to what had gone before, both issues were productive of early and satisfactory results.

The passing of the Conciliation and Arbitration Act followed upon a classic instance of political horse-trading. A deputation from the unions met Forrest while the congress was still in session and sought to extract from him the promise that the bill would be re-introduced without delay. Forrest used the occasion to solve a problem connected with his own political future. It was generally accepted that colonial premiers would be offered cabinet posts in the new federal government and Forrest wished to remain premier until the federal elections were held in 1901. However his popularity in the Legislative Assembly had begun to decline and it seemed likely that a proposed vote of no-confidence in his premiership would succeed. In a private meeting with the deputation the premier therefore offered to introduce the bill, provided labour used its influence to dissuade those who intended voting against him from doing so.[82] A bargain was struck, the deputation reported back to Congress and the meeting then resolved:

> That in the opinion of this Congress, any MP who, by voting to close this session, or otherwise tries to block the passage, or who fails to support, when introduced, the Compulsory Conciliation and Arbitration Act, will be looked upon as an enemy of the Labour interest.[83]

The resolution amounted to an instruction that Forrest should not be ousted, for the business of changing governments would prevent an arbitration bill from being passed for some time. The no-confidence motion admittedly was not withdrawn, but there were members in the Assembly who were either sympathetic to labour, or else could not afford to incur the political hostility of the labour movement, and their votes gave Forrest the support he needed to defeat the motion.[84] With this the passage of the act was assured. Introduced in August 1900, it passed on to the Statute Book on 5 December in the same year, becoming the earliest example in Australian history of the official acceptance of the principle of compulsory arbitration.[85]

It might well seem that this undoubted advance in labour's standing owed more to political expediency than it did to the urgings of congress. But so to construe these events is to understate the power which the unions were coming to possess. That they could have induced Forrest to treat with them and have influenced crucial votes in the Legislative Assembly indicates that they were now a force to be reckoned with, and there can be little doubt that it was the growing convergence of the movements on the goldfields and on the coast that had given them this strength.

The Conciliation and Arbitration Act set out to create a collective bargaining system. It intended that everything should be done through associations, and neither employer nor worker could approach the court except through officers of their association. As a result it converted the union from a purely voluntary combination to an organisation which was indispensable to the proper administration of the law. Unions could be formed by employers or employees and it was necessary for them to be registered and to file annual returns of membership and funds. Employers' unions were required to have a minimum membership of five persons residing in the colony, and workers' unions a membership of fifteen.

Under the act all disputes had first to go before a Board of Conciliation, and it was only if the board was unable to settle the dispute that it was brought before the Court of Arbitration. The court was composed of three members, one appointed by the employers, one by the unions and one by the governor, with the governor's nominee being a judge of the Supreme Court. The proceedings of the court were conclusive and final. It had the power to enforce its awards and where an award was breached a penalty of up to £500 could be imposed on offenders.[86]

A necessary prerequisite to the operation of the Conciliation and Arbitration Act was the legalisation of the trade union and of the activities normally associated with it. As the law then stood both were illegal and the act was technically unworkable until the change in legal status was effected. The unions had long campaigned for recognition and a demand for legalisation had been included in the resolutions unsuccessfully put up by the first Trades and Labour Congress. Now in 1900 this objective was at last achieved, without any special effort on their part, as a necessary corollary to the arbitration bill. Legalisation came in two stages. A Conspiracy and Protection of Property Act which declared trade union activities to be lawful was passed in conjunction with the arbitration bill in December 1900, and two years later the passage of a Trade Union Regulation Act resolved doubts as to whether trade unions could legally register under the arbitration bill.[87] When this second piece of legislation was assented to in February 1902 trade unionism finally became a recognised part of the life of the Western Australian community.

The Second Congress's drive for greater political representation at both state and federal levels was not restricted by the financial impediments of earlier times. The passing of the Payment of Members Act in the colonial legislature in 1900 and the acceptance of the principle that federal members of parliament should be remunerated removed a major hurdle to labour representation in both institutions. What was needed now was an effective political organisation, and as the leaders on the goldfields were still divided over the details of the proposed Australian Labour Federation the unionists fell back on an extended version of the old coastal Political Labour Party. The latter set up a number of branches on both the goldfields and the coast, opening membership to non-unionists who sympathised with the movement's ideals. Candidates were run in both federal and state elections, and in comparison with its previous performances, the P.L.P. did remarkably well. Two places in the Senate and two seats in the House of Representatives was its tally in the federal poll, and in the state election the party came out with six seats.[88] An analysis of the voting in the state contest showed the validity of the case for electoral redistribution. Six Labour members polled 9,658 votes, while the government party with nineteen members polled only 7,549.[89]

Union Problems and Policies in the 20th Century

An issue which gained a considerable degree of prominence in the trade union world during these last years of the 1890s was that concerning the immigration of coloured labour. Objections to the practice had been voiced from time to time over the course of the nineteenth century,[90] but an organised campaign did not appear until the labour movement got under way. In 1892 a public meeting condemning such immigration was staged by prominent coastal unionists, who held that the continued entry of Asians would lead to competition and lower wages and was therefore 'detrimental to the interests of the white working class.' These arguments, which were largely directed against the Chinese, were embodied in a petition to parliament, but with no result, since the northern pastoral representatives did not think it in their interest to support it. The campaign continued unabated, and within a year the coastal unionists found new allies on the goldfields, where the introduction of Afghan camel drivers, who quickly established a monopoly over the carrying trade, had begun to arouse strong feelings. The combined weight of the goldfields and coastal anti-Asian activity was sufficient to initiate legislation curbing Chinese immigration in 1897, but the other categories of coloured labour continued to enter unimpeded.[91] The fight against Asian immigration then became part of the official trade union political labour programmes. It figured as a plank in the election platform of the Political Progressive League in 1898, in the several resolutions passed by the First and Second Trade Union Congresses in 1899 and 1900, and was part of the programme with which labour went to the polls in the federal election of 1900. However, the immigration issue did not long remain the exclusive concern of the labour movement. By the end of the century hostility to Asian immigration had become widespread in all the Australian colonies, and opponents of the existing policy were to be found at all levels of the population. It was this consensus of general opinion and not the influence of any single group that finally settled the question in 1901, by inspiring the passage of the Immigration Restriction Act during the first session of the new federal parliament.

The disagreements on the goldfields which arose in the early years of the twentieth century stemmed directly from the organisational experiments of the A.W.A. In its enthusiasm for large-scale, open-door unionism, the A.W.A. overstepped the mark and began to include the self-employed within its ranks. In addition, it contended that its composite organisation was adequate to protect and control all workers on the fields and that the division of unionism into a series of lowest common denominations was a menace to the cause of labour in Western Australia. This precipitated a clash with the craft unions in the Goldfields Trades and Labour Council and after an acrimonious exchange of views culminated in the A.W.A.'s withdrawal from the council in November 1900.[92] Worse was to follow. In a matter of weeks the A.W.A. found itself with an internal revolt on its hands. A group of union 'purists' drawn from the mining sector took exception to the extension of membership to non-wage earners, and led by Jabez Dodd broke away in 1901 to set up the Australian Miners Association.[93] The new union, which grew rapidly, commenced a running battle with the A.W.A., which became the trade union movement's most serious conflict between 1900 and 1907.

The points at issue between the two organisations went well beyond the immediate cause of the rift. In contrast to the A.W.A.'s composite membership, the A.M.A. only organised underground miners. Again, the A.W.A. laid emphasis upon union participation in all possible political arenas, whereas the A.M.A. argued that purely political organisations rather than unions should represent the workers' political interests. Sectarianism seems to have been another divisive influence. Dodd and many other leading members of the A.M.A. were Methodists of Welsh, Cornish and northern English descent, while the A.W.A. seemed to attract Scottish and Irish Catholics.[94] These sectarian rivalries were exacerbated as they were elsewhere in Australia at this time, by differences of opinion over the Irish home rule question. At first the breach between the unions did not lead to serious discord within the trade union movement as a whole but as time went on the A.M.A. began to challenge A.W.A. branch registrations under the Arbitration Act and this set off a fierce demarcation battle which for a time undermined working class unity on the goldfields.[95]

Though the unions had won the principle of compulsory arbitration, they were less than satisfied with several clauses in the bill. Their main objections centred on the definition of the word 'worker,' which excluded clerical and government employees from the benefits of the act; on the need to pay a deposit before making reference to the Arbitration Court; on the permission granted to lawyers to practice in the court, and on the lack of a provision for a quorum of less than the full court of three members.[96] That some of these objections were not misplaced soon became apparent. A few months after the arbitration system went into operation a dispute in the Railway Department developed into a serious strike because the railway union had a large number of clerical workers on its rolls and was unable to register under the act. Again, at about the same time the employer's representative on the Arbitration Court went off on an engineering job to Broken Hill, and owing to the lack of a quorum the court was paralysed for a number of months.[97]

The opportunity to amend the bill came Labor's way during the chaotic period that followed Forrest's appointment to the federal ministry. Four premiers, George Throssell, George Leake, Alfred Morgans and then Leake again, held office between February and December 1901. The second Leake government was dependent on the support of the P.L.P., and with the premier himself in favour of amendment, Labor was able to engineer a number of important changes to the bill. The Amendment Act of 1902 overcame many of the unionists' earlier objections. Clerks and government workers were brought within the operation of the act; lawyers were permitted in the Arbitration Court only if both parties to a dispute agreed; and the condition that reference to the court be accompanied by the payment of a deposit, was done away with. An important innovation was also made on the penal side. The framers of the original act appear to have assumed that all industrial associations would register as a matter of course, and that strikes and lockouts would be avoided thereafter by the clause which made awards compulsory. However for one reason or another a number of associations failed to register and the continuance of strikes and lockouts remained a distinct possibility. To meet this contingency the amending act declared all strikes and lockouts illegal and persons guilty of initiating such action were made liable to a fine of up to £25.[98]

A section of the act from which much had been expected was that establishing conciliation boards. It was believed that the boards would handle most disputes, with only the more serious going before the court. In practice the right of appeal to the Arbitration Court from the findings of the board undermined its usefulness, and in the three years 1901-03, of twenty-five cases dealt with by the board, fifteen were subsequently referred to the court. This made it evident that the boards were not serving any useful purpose and after 1903 no further disputes were taken before them.[99]

The introduction of the arbitration bills had two immediate consequences in the trade union world. One was that the number of unions and of union members grew rapidly as previously unorganised groups of workers sought access to the benefits of arbitration by registering under the act. The other was that unionisation on sectional lines was encouraged by a clause in the 1902 bill which sought to prevent an unnecessary proliferation of unions by insisting that thereafter there should be only one union to each occupation.[100] This established a primacy of craft organisations over those preferring a more general membership and had such dire effects on the multi-vocational A.W.A. that its very nature was transformed. The branches it set up after 1902 had to restructure themselves into separate vocational unions before they could register under the act. Multi-vocational branches registered before 1902 were not declared invalid, but where these included miners their registrations were often successfully challenged by the A.M.A., it being held by the court that the latter was the first union to register specifically for that occupation.[101] The decline in strength and influence of the A.W.A. dates from this time. Its dispute with the A.M.A. was ultimately settled in 1906 when the Western Federated Miners Union was set up, but that was a further defeat since the new federation reflected the organisational philosophy of its rival.[102] Membership dwindled with every passing year, and by the end of the decade the once powerful A.W.A. was but a shadow of its former self.

The extension of unionism in the early years of the twentieth century had notable repercussions on labour's political wing. Further trade union congresses in 1901 and 1902 had attempted to resurrect the A.L.F. proposal, though without success. The coastal and goldfields unions were as yet too wary of one another, and the dispute between the A.M.A. and the A.W.A. too bitter, for the plan to take root. The approach of the federal election of 1903 brought fresh attempts to resurrect the scheme, and ultimately a federation of sorts was launched by the executives of the coastal and goldfields T.L.C.s and of some of the larger unions. Its efforts were impressively successful; Labour won four of the five seats in the House of Representatives, and all three seats in the Senate. Yet, the federation proved to be nothing more than an organisational expedient for fighting the election. The old antagonisms surfaced again, suggestions that the arrangement be made permanent were brushed aside, and the strategy was shelved immediately the election was over.[103]

That the successes of the federal campaign could be repeated at state level was fast becoming evident by 1904. The rapid penetration of the unions had widened Labour's electoral base and the James government, which Labour had helped to keep in office, had abolished plural and property voting and had brought about a redistribution of parliamentary seats, which gave the goldfields a more equitable representation. Seeing that there was little likelihood of the A.L.F. being re-established, Labour decided to fight the forthcoming state election through the P.L.P., and to contest as many seats as possible. The results were dramatic. Five of the sitting Labour members were unopposed and of the twenty-eight other seats contested seventeen were won with 42.5 per cent of the total vote. The party emerged as the largest single group in the house, and on 10 August 1904, with the support of five Independents, Western Australia's first Labour government was set up under Henry Daglish.[104] The programme on which the election was fought was relatively innocuous. Abolition of the Legislative Council, state control of the liquor trade, a tax on unimproved land values, a state-owned banking and insurance system — these were not burning public issues. James's electoral reforms appear to have contributed far more to Labour's success than did the party programme. Daglish's minority government lasted barely a year but all the same its election was a benchmark in the state's history. Like the industrial wing before it, Labour's political wing had served notice that it was henceforth to play a major role in the affairs of the community.

A series of events which followed upon Labour's political

baptism prepared the ground for the permanent establishment of the A.L.F. The apprehension with which the coastal and goldfields sections of the movement had viewed one another began to disappear as the decline in mining after 1903 brought a lessening in the influence of the goldfields' unions. On the goldfields themselves the settling of the dispute between the A.M.A. and the A.W.A. led to an increasing sense of cohesion, and an economic recession which began in 1905 so reduced union membership and finances that a recasting of their organisational structure became imperative. The sum of these forces led first to the A.L.F. being reconstituted to fight the federal election of 1906, and then to the decision of the Trades and Labour Congress of 1907 that the A.L.F. be made permanent. The structure of the federation differed substantially from that originally proposed at the first Trades and Labour Congress. It was governed by a general council which met every three years, and in the interim periods its business was conducted by an executive composed of council nominees and of delegates from a number of district councils. The district councils were made up of delegates from the unions and political branches within each district and were the grass-roots of the federation. They performed the role of unifying the industrial and political activities of the labour movement, and so effectively was this done that within two years the T.L.C.s on the coast and on the goldfields had merged with the metropolitan and goldfields' district councils respectively.[105] The setting up of the A.L.F. was thus a most eventful step. It wrought a fundamental change in the organisational pattern of the trade union movement by replacing a purely industrial coordinating body, in the shape of the T.L.C., with one in which the pure politician had an equal place. Furthermore the manner in which this was done completed the fusion of the labour movements on the coast and the goldfields by making them components of a wider organisation.

With the founding of the A.L.F. one comes to the end of what might be called the formative years of Western Australian trade unionism. By 1907 unionism was legal, was well organised, had many adherents, was accepted by the public, and had a well-developed political wing. Moreover, the movement had by then acquired certain characteristics which were to persist and grow as the years went by. Of these the principle of arbitration was perhaps the most important. It rapidly acquired a major influence over trade union activity, and if there were occasions thereafter when faith in its efficacy seemed to waver, these were only temporary aberrations of little significance. The use of the principle had a conditioning effect on the composition and tactics of the union world. It encouraged the growth of the craft union at the expense of the broader association and it bred a pragmatic short-term approach to the leading industrial issues of the day.

Similarly, the A.L.F. provided the labour movement with a framework which made it unique in Australia. In the eastern states the political Labor Parties and representative tradè union bodies maintained their separate identities, but in Western Australia both trade union and political activities were controlled by the district councils of a single statewide organisation. These arrangements lasted for over fifty years, and during that time Western Australia possessed the most integrated labour movement in the world.

The new relationship between trade union and political party had a substantial impact on the class composition and outlook of the labour movement. Throughout the nineties 'trade unionism' and 'the labour movement' were synonymous terms, and such political action as was undertaken was firmly controlled by the T.L.C. That a strong working-class outlook emerged during this period is perceptible in the incidents surrounding the lumpers' strike, and in the views expressed at the early trade union congresses. The expansion of the P.L.P. in 1901, with its policy of admitting to membership sympathisers who were neither unionists nor members of the working class had the effect of dividing the labour movement into two quite distinct sections, and of diffusing the class composition of its political wing. Nevertheless, these changes were not then of particular significance since the numbers involved on the political side were small and since the separate identity of the unions left them in charge of their own affairs. The founding of the A.L.F. pushed the process of diffusion a great deal further. Not only did it increase the non-unionist, non-working-class component of the labour movement, it gave that component a considerable say in trade union matters by so merging the political and industrial wings as to eliminate the T.L.C. and establish a system of common control via the district councils. Given these developments it is not surprising that the class consciousness of earlier times was quickly blunted and that it came to be replaced by a practical, matter of fact approach which combined well with the pragmatism encouraged by the arbitration bill.

The relatively peaceful manner in which the Western Australian unions achieved so many of their objectives is in marked contrast to labour's experience in the East. There, the 1890s were years of bitter confrontation and defeat which threatened on occasion to destroy the union movement. General economic expansion in the West, as against slump and contraction elsewhere, might seem adequately to explain the difference, but such reasoning would altogether neglect the role played by Sir John Forrest. It was Forrest's use of those prosperous conditions to make concessions to labour that produced the more harmonious relationships of the West.

So far as political philosophy went, the union movement continued to profess a commitment to socialism. Whether the term had the connotations that now attach to it however, is open to doubt. Admittedly there were unionists and labour politicians, both on the goldfields and on the coast, who understood and supported the theoretical implications of scientific socialism, but they were relatively few in number. Most leaders and the majority of the rank and file seem to have had only the vaguest idea as to what socialism actually involved. To some, it meant state enterprise, though in certain selected areas alone, and not as part of an integrated plan. To others, it represented a concern for the welfare of the weak and the underprivileged. To most, it was a system which assured the working man of a fair return for his labours, and guaranteed to him a general standard of living that was worthy of a human being. This last interpretation was not without its religious overtones, for it was widely believed that there was a minimum level to which every citizen of a Christian society was entitled.[106] This belief is no where better expressed than in these few lines taken from the labour press:

> I cannot eat my daily bread alone,
> Send none to me if these cannot be fed,
> With them I stand or fall, for we are one,
> Father gives all of us our daily bread.[107]

REFERENCES

1. *Census of Western Australia,* 1870, pp. 33, 38-39.
2. *Ibid.* 1881, p. 30.
3. *Blue Book of Western Australia,* 1870, p. 64.
4. F.K. Crowley, "Master and Servant in Western Australia, 1851-1901," *Western Australian Historical Society Journal and Proceedings* 4, 6 (1954), p. 17.
5. W. Somerville, 'An Economic History of Western Australia' (MS. deposited at the Reid Library, University of Western Australia), Vol. 2, p. 305; B. Smith, 'Early Western Australian Literature,' *University Studies in History* IV, 1 (1961/62), p. 47.
6. Somerville, pp. 306-8; T.A. Coghlan, *Labour and Industry in Australia* (Melbourne, 1969), Vol. III, pp. 1566-68; *Western Australian Year Book,* 1902-4, p. 286.
7. Coghlan, p. 1567; H.J. Gibbney, 'Working class Organisation in Western Australia, 1880-1902' (B.A. Hons. thesis, University of Western Australia, 1949), pp. 2-3.
8. C.T. Stannage, 'Electoral Politics in Western Australia 1884-1897' (M.A. thesis, University of Western Australia, 1967).
9. Gibbney, p. 3.
10. Somerville, p. 305; Gibbney, pp. 3-4.
11. *Census of Western Australia,* 1881, pp. 86-88.
12. Somerville, pp. 306-7, Gibbney, pp. 4-5, 8-9.
13. Crowley, p. 23.
14. Coghlan, p. 1569; Gibbney, pp. 6-10; Stannage, pp. 111-18.
15. Coghlan, p. 1572; Somerville, p. 311; *West Australian* (henceforth *W.A.*) 6-7-1889, p. 3.
16. Coghlan, p. 1569.
17. *W.A.,* 6-2-1886, p. 3; 18-2-1886, p. 3; 29-7-1886, p. 3.
18. Gibbney, p. 11.
19. *W.A.,* 30-10-1889, p. 3.
20. Coghlan, p. 1573.
21. Gibbney, pp. 11-12; Stannage, pp. 116-17.

22. Coghlan, p. 1574.
23. *Ibid.*
24. *Ibid.*, pp. 1574-75.
25. *Western Australian Year Book*, 1902-4, p. 1152.
26. *Ibid.*, p. 311; *Blue Book of Western Australia*, 1891, p. 201.
27. Gibbney, pp. 179-80; Somerville, p. 318; Coghlan, p. 1576.
28. Somerville, p. 318A; Gibbney, pp. 16-17.
29. Coghlan, p. 1576; Stannage, p. 119.
30. Gibbney, p. 17.
31. *Ibid.* p. 20; Somerville, pp. 335-35A. .
32. Coghlan, p. 1579.
33. Stannage, p. 121.
34. *Ibid.*, p. 122.
35. *Ibid.*, pp. 125-28.
36. *Ibid.*, p. 128; see also Gibbney, p. 24.
37. H.J. Gibbney, 'Western Australia,' in D.J. Murphy (ed.), *Labour in Politics* (St Lucia, 1975), p. 346.
38. Gibbney, 'Working Class Organisation,' pp. 183-85.
39. L.B. McIntyre, 'The development of trade unionism in Western Australia and the operation of industrial conciliation and arbitration, 1900-1914' (M.A. thesis, University of Western Australia, 1972), pp. 23-24.
40. Crowley, pp. 26-28; J. Merritt, 'George Foster Pearce – Labour Leader' (M.A. thesis, University of Western Australia, 1963).
41. Gibbney, 'Working Class Organisation,' pp. 117-19.
42. Stannage, p. 131.
43. *W.A.*, 15-10-1892, p. 5; 8-11-1892, p. 3.
44. *W.A.*, 3-8-1892, p. 4.
45. Gibbney, 'Working Class Organisation,' pp. 22-23.
46. *Ibid.*, p. 28; Coghlan, Vol. 4, p. 2076.
47. Coghlan, p. 2077; for a detailed discussion see J. Merritt, 'George Foster Pearce and the Building Trades Strike of 1897,' *Bulletin of the Australian Society for the Study of Labour History* 3 (November 1962) pp. 5, 22.
48. *W.A.*, 16-2-1899, p. 2; 17-2-1899, p. 7.
49. *W.A.*, 20-2-1899, pp. 1, 7.
50. *W.A.*, 21-2-1899, p. 1.
51. *W.A.*, 23-2-1899, p. 2.
52. *W.A.*, 7-3-1899, p. 5.
53. *W.A.*, 16-3-1899, p. 5; 27-3-1899, p. 5.
54. *W.A.*, 3-4-1899, p. 6.

55. *W.A.*, 9-3-1899, p. 5.
56. A list of donations was published for the first time in the *West Australian* of 13-3-1899, p. 5, and further lists appeared at regular intervals thereafter.
57. Gibbney, 'Working Class Organization,' pp. 30-34; Coghlan, pp. 2081-82.
58. Somerville, p. 357.
59. Gibbney, "Working Class Organisation,' p. 54.
60. *Ibid.*; McIntyre, pp. 22-23.
61. D. Mossenon, 'Mining Regulations and Alluvial Disputes, 1894-1904,' *University Studies in History II*, 3 (September 1955), p. 12; Gibbney, 'Working Class Organisation,' p. 53; Somerville, p. 365.
62. Mossenson, pp. 18-19.
63. Gibbney, 'Working Class Organisation,' p. 54.
64. McIntyre, pp. 24-25; Somerville, p. 438; Gibbney, 'Working Class Organisation,' p. 36.
65. *Statistical Register of Western Australia* 1910, Part VII, p. 6.
66. *Ibid.*, 1914, Part I, p. 5.
67. *Ibid.*, 1908, Part IV, p. 287.
68. *Ibid.*, 1910. Part Vi, p. 22.
69. McIntyre, p. 293.
70. *Ibid.*, Table 18.
71. Commonwealth Bureau of Census and Statistics, *Labour Report* No. 2, p. 12.
72. Somerville, p. 379; Coghlan, p. 2307; Mossenson, p. 29.
73. *W.A.*, 11-4-1899, pp. 6, 7.
74. *W.A.*, 15-4-1899, p. 7.
75. *W.A.*, 12-4-1899, p. 6; 15-4-1899, p. 7.
76. Gibbney, 'Working Class Organisation,' p. 88.
77. Gibbney, 'Western Australia,' p. 349.
78. Gibbney, ' Working Class Organisation', p. 121; Western Australian *Parliamentary Debates (W.A.P.D.)* XIV, pp. 1174-87.
79. *W.A.P.D.*, XI, 1897, p. 91; J. Merritt, 'George Foster Pearce and the Western Australian Labour Movement; 1892-1901,' *University Studies in History* 4, 3 (1965), p. 65.
80. *W.A.P.D.*, XIV, 1899, pp. 1169, 1172, 1324, 2928.
81. *W.A.*, 17-10-1900, p. 5; Somerville, pp. 418, 438.
82. Somerville, p. 433; Merritt, 'Pearce – Labour Leader,' pp. 138-39.
83. *W.A.*, 17-8-1900, p. 7.
84. Merritt, 'Pearce – Labour Leader,' p. 352.

85. *Acts of the Parliament of Western Australia*, August to December 1900, pp. 425-58.
86. *Ibid.*
87. *Ibid.*, pp. 419-23.
88. *W.A.P.D.*, 19, pp. 730-33.
89. Gibbney, 'Western Australia,' p. 352.
90. *W.A.*, 25-11-1883 (editorial); The People 2-1-1892, p. 9.
91. Gibbney, 'Working Class Organisation,' pp. 152-57; Somerville, p. 429.
92. Gibbney, 'Working Class Organisation,' p. 58.
93. Somerville, pp. 364-66A; *Westralian Worker* 11-1-1901, p. 5.
94. Somerville, pp. 364-66A.
95. McIntyre, p. 70.
96. Merritt, 'Pearce – Labour Leader,' p. 141; McIntyre, p. 126; J. Wittenoom, 'The Growth of Industrial Arbitration in Western Australia' (B.A. Hons. thesis, University of Western Australia, 1948, p. 20.
97. McIntyre, p. 127; Somerville, p. 466.
98. *Acts of the Parliament of Western Australia*, 1901-02, pp. 533-74.
99. Somerville, p. 466; McIntyre, p. 127; J.S. Battye (ed.), *Cyclopedia of Western Australia*, 2 Vols. (Adelaide, 1912 and 1913), p. 715.
100. *V and P 1903-04*, Vol. II, No. 22.
101. McIntyre, pp. 155-59.
102. *Ibid.*, pp. 92-93.
103. Gibbney, 'Western Australia,' pp. 354-55; C.A. Hughes and B.D. Graham, *A Handbook of Australian Government and Politics, 1890-1964* (Canberra, 1968), p. 295.
104. Gibbney, 'Western Australia,' p. 356.
105. *Ibid.* p. 361; McIntyre, pp. 90-92.
106. These several interpretations of socialism are apparent in various issues of the *Westralian Worker*. A number of relevant quotations have been brought together by Gibbney in 'Working Class Organisation,' Chap. 4.
107. Gibbney, 'Working Class Organisation,' p. 88.

2

Confrontation and Reconciliation on the Waterfront: The Fremantle Lumpers Strike – 1899

It is a notable feature of Western Australian labour history that the Fremantle lumpers' strike of 1899 has not been given the prominence it deserves. In the published literature the most exhaustive account of the strike barely totals a page and a half,[1] and in unpublished research the coverage though somewhat wider is far from adequate.[2] There is no denying the importance of the strike. It was of five weeks duration, the longest major strike Western Australia had yet experienced; it occurred in an employment which was of vital importance to a geographically isolated colony; it served as a classic example of the growing confrontation between organised labour and organised capital; it made apparent the Government's hostility to early unionism, and its willingness to connive at its destruction; it reflected a rising sense of solidarity in the Western Australian working class; it succeeded in making the union an indisputable fact on the waterfront; and above all, it did much to convince the public that arbitration was a viable instrument of industrial reconciliation.

The origins of the strike of 1899 can be traced to a series of events which had taken place some two and a half years earlier. In 1896 the demands of a rapidly increasing population together with an extended programme of public works and the gold discoveries of the year before combined to bring about a dramatic increase in trade.[3] The carrying services of the colony were soon under extreme pressure and the port of Fremantle grew so congested that 'some articles which had been brought to the colony in abundance were selling in Perth at double their ordinary price because the wharves could not be cleared.'[4]

The port lumpers were not slow to recognise the advantages inherent in such a situation. They had been dissatisfied for some time with rates of pay which they thought inadequate because of the irregularity of their work and the high cost of living. Their Union now asked that the hourly rate for ordinary day work be raised from 1s. to 1s. 3d., and overtime from 1s. 6d. to 2s. Given the circumstances the shipping companies had no alternative but to agree to these demands.[5] The concession, however, was no more than a temporary expedient and the employers bided their time until economic conditions altered sufficiently to shift the balance of bargaining power in their favour.[6]

It was in the middle of 1898 that the labour market began to move in a direction which favoured the employer. In the main this was due to a fundamental change in the nature of goldmining. By the second half of the 1890s alluvial gold had begun to run out and extraction from deeper seams required the use of capital equipment which most prospectors could not afford. Some then became employees of goldmining companies while others drifted back to Perth and Fremantle looking for employment.[7] A rapid decline in immigration accompanied these changes, and it was not long before trade in the coastal towns began to feel the effects of the contraction in consumer demand. This helped to swell the ranks of the unemployed and it was claimed that by early 1899 between 2,000 and 3,000 persons were out of work in Perth and Fremantle[8] and that of these 'some were absolutely starving.'[9]

Shipping companies concerned with the intercolonial trade, which accounted for two-thirds of the shipping calling at Fremantle, had come together in the West Australian Steamship Owners Association, and it was the action which they now took that precipitated the lumpers' strike.

On 15 February the Shipping Association posted a notice at the office of the Adelaide Steamship Company which set out the terms under which maritime labour was to be hired as from 1 March. The notice, signed by the AUSN Company, the Adelaide Steamship Company, Hoddart Parker and Co. Pty. Ltd., W. Howard Smith and Sons Ltd., McIlwraith, McEacharn and Co. Pty. Ltd., and the Melbourne Steamship Company Ltd.,[10] adversely affected every facet of employment of the port labourers. In effect this meant that the former could hire whom they wished when they wished, and so scotched any hope that the Union may have had of maintaining a closed shop on the waterfront. Moreover, the stevedores were to decide the number of men in each labour gang. This new arrangement was in sharp contrast to previous practice whereby the Union had been a party to that decision, and was clearly intended to undermine the standing of the Union. This was made doubly clear by the chairman of the Association when in a statement to the press he insisted that the employers did not recognise the Union and would have no dealings with it. Secondly, the working day was set at eight hours, to fall between 6 a.m. and 6 p.m. on weekdays. Previously, the work day had fallen between 8 a.m. and 5 p.m., all other hours being overtime. This meant that gangs starting work at 6 a.m., if obliged by the nature of the job they were engaged upon to work through into the night, would not be eligible for extra pay until after 6 p.m. in the evening, and so were losers of the equivalent of three hours overtime. Thirdly, rates of pay were reduced all round. The rate for ordinary time was to be 1s. 1½d. instead of 1s. 3d., and for overtime 1s. 8d. per hour was to be allowed in lieu of 2s. Again, under the old agreement 2s. 6d. an hour was allowed for work on holidays and 4s. an hour on Sundays, but on and after 1 March the Association decided to allow a flat rate of 2s. 3d. an hour for both holidays and Sundays. The new scales were only marginally better than those in operation before 1896 and were thus a serious erosion of the gains made by the lumpers in that year. Fourthly, an innovation was introduced in regard to coaling. Gangs were in future to be paid by tonnage at 9d. a ton for day work, 1s. 1½d. a ton overtime, and 1s. 6d. a ton on Sundays and holidays. The new day rate was a full 6d. a ton lower than that current in Albany and represented a reduction of over 36 per cent on the existing remuneration for working coal.[11] Finally, all hours of labour were to be reckoned from the time the men actually arrived on the ships they were scheduled to work. Time spent travelling to and from ships which were not anchored alongside the wharf was to be paid for at a rate of 6d. an hour, and the full day rate was to apply only for the time actually worked. This last provision represented a further reduction in the lumpers' earnings, for ships often anchored in Gage Roads, Careening Bay, Owen Anchorage, and Rockingham, and did so, it must be emphasised, to suit the convenience of the shipping agents. The Shipping Association did not inform the Union of these proposed changes, for to have done so would have implied recognition. Instead, the men were informed individually by their several employers, and through notices posted up at the Company offices.[12]

The Shipping Association did not think it necessary to justify its action. In an interview with the press the president merely observed that the new regulations 'were the rules under which the Association would in future work,' and that he had 'nothing to state in regard to the new rules or the reason which led to their promulgation.'[13] The lumpers, however, did not need an explanation. The weakness of their economic standing was apparent to them and as one of their representatives put it: 'Unquestionably the time is a favourable one for the steamship owners to seek to reduce wages. The lumpers are pretty well starved down at the present time, and are to a large extent in the power of their employers.'[14]

It was not with the Shipping Association alone that the lumpers had to contend. Another opponent was the State Government, which because of earlier events was also interested in lowering wages on the waterfront. Through its ownership of the railways the Government was the employer of a type of wharf labour known as truckers. It was the truckers' job to load and unload the railway wagons which moved cargo between the warehouses and the wharves. Under existing arrangements they were paid by the Railway Department for ordinary day labour, and by the steamship companies whenever overtime was worked, at rates similar to those paid to the lumpers. These scales had been set in 1896, when the

Lumpers Union took truckers into its ranks so as to establish a uniform rate on the waterfront. This uniformity was broken in 1899 when the Steamship Owners Association issued its new regulations. It was declared that the truckers were henceforth to receive less all round than the lumpers, the proposed rates being 1s. an hour for day work, 1s. 6d. an hour overtime, and 2s. an hour on holidays and Sundays. To the Union it seemed strange that a private body should announce a change in Government wage scales, and when it was discovered that J.T. Short, the Chief Traffic Manager of the railways, had been present at the Association's meeting, it was quick to condemn 'the subtle manner in which the application of the reductions to Government employees was being secured.'[15] The occupations of lumper and trucker, it was held, required the same measure of skill, and it seemed that the Government was conniving with the steamship companies to undermine the Union by driving a wedge between lumpers and truckers.

On the whole, however, the initial reaction was remarkable muted. Union officials did not even summon a meeting of the membership and were content merely to voice their criticisms in the press. A fortnight had still to elapse before the revised regulations took effect, and the unionists may well have thought that they had ample time in which to plan a counter strategy. If any such illusions existed, they were quickly dispelled. Two days later, on Saturday 18 February, the steamship companies advertised for labourers willing to work on the new terms. The most significant part of the notice was its concluding sentences which said that preference would be given to old employees provided they registered their names *before 12 noon on the following Monday.*[16]

There can be little doubt that the advertisement was meant to hasten the men into applying for re-employment, and to spur them on with the veiled threat that replacements would otherwise be found. What it succeeded in doing was to galvanise the Union into action. A meeting was hurriedly called the next day and a counter strategy drawn up. It was decided that the main issue at stake was the recognition of the Union, since this would in turn facilitate negotiations over wages and working hours. Accordingly, it was resolved that recognition would have to be conceded before any discussions began, and that in the meantime no Union member should respond to the Association's advertisement.[17] This was tantamount to a declaration of hostilities, for it meant that the shipping companies would inevitably have to employ non-union men.

When the deadline was reached on Monday, none of the old employees had signed on.[18] The Association's response was to change course somewhat by substituting overt inducements for covert threats. Yet another advertisement was posted to announce that Labour Bureaux had been set up in Perth and Fremantle for the recruitment of lumpers and that *permanent* employment could be obtained by experienced men. These permanent hands were to be paid at regulation rates, i.e. 48s. a week plus overtime whether fully employed or not, and were to have written agreements for one month with the option of renewal for a longer period.[19] To many a lumper, accustomed at best to a three day week, these terms must have seemed most attractive. Yet none succumbed to the temptation, and that they did not is indicative of the degree of solidarity and conviction which imbued the Union.

It was at this point that the Trades and Labour Council took an interest in the problems of the lumpers and truckers. But there was little the Council could do, beyond pledging support for the Union, condemning the Government's role, and authorising a delegation to seek an interview with the Commissioner of Railways.[20] A week had still to elapse before the revisions took effect and the Council, like the lumpers, truckers, Steamship Owners Association and Government, had to await 1 March.

Tension began to mount as the end of February approached. The Association continued its daily advertisements and claimed that applications, though not necessarily from experienced men, were flowing in.[21] The unionists made it known that they would present themselves for work on the 1st expecting payment at the old rates. A refusal to employ them on those terms would, they argued, amount to a lock-out. 'We claim that we are not striking. We simply refuse to accept the reductions in wages which the Steamship Owners Association has arbitrarily made.'[22]

The 1st March proved something of an anti-climax. Theoretically, the strike (or lock-out) commenced, but all was quiet on the wharves as there were no ships belonging to the Association in port. The Labour Bureaux put twenty of their new recruits to work unloading a permanent coal hulk belonging to the Adelaide Steamship Company, but most of the men 'threw in the sponge' before the day was out, the work being extremely fatiguing.[23] The lumpers, who had earlier given an assurance that law and order would be observed, made no attempt to interfere with these operations. Nevertheless, the Police Department sent down a number of reinforcements, even though the inspector-in-charge at Fremantle had made no such request. The Government was now involved in the dispute through the Railway Department and evidently the police were there to aid in the enforcement of the new regulations.[24]

It was a different story where the truckers were concerned. A confrontation between the Railway Department and its employees began on the morning of the 1st and started off a chain of events which makes it evident that the strike of 1899 was in reality two strikes in one.[25]

Soon after the change in wage scales had been announced, the Railway Department took a further step which can only be looked upon as a subtle attempt to intimidate the truckers. On the 20th February the Department decided to convert into permanent employees labourers who had been employed casually in the goods sheds. Wages were set at 48s. a week plus overtime and an important part of the agreement was that the new recruits could be put to work in the trucks if necessary. In justifying this change in stance the Department claimed that it had been decided some twelve months earlier that permanent hands should be employed as truckers, but that 'for some reason' the scheme had not been put into effect and that this was now being done.[26]

That the proposal was an old one is true, but as the secretary of the Lumpers Union observed, 'it was peculiar that the matter should be revived at this particular juncture, when there was trouble between the Union and the Steamship Owners Association.'[27] Certainly, it gave credence to the charge that there was collusion between the Department and the Association. The implementation of the plan at just that time seemed intended to strengthen the cause of the steamship owners by weakening the forces that opposed them. Truckers who had joined the Union were to be penalised by having their jobs taken away and offered to permanent hands in the goods sheds. Presumably it was hoped that the new appointees would take note of what had occurred and realise that there were hazards associated with Union membership.

Despite this move the Railway Department was unable to recruit a sufficient number of permanent hands of the required quality before the end of February and so had to shift its ground yet again. On the morning of 1 March, the regular truckers were sent for and offered permanent employment on the same terms as those given the workers in the goods sheds. The offer was an attractive one, for though the rates were similar to the revisions proposed by the Steamship Owners Association, permanency of employment ensured higher weekly earnings than casual labour did. Nevertheless, a sense of loyalty to their allies on the waterfront led the truckers to refuse immediate acceptance of the scheme. They declared that they would be 'only too willing' to accept the new terms but not 'until the present trouble with the lumpers was over.'[28]

After this rebuff, the Railway Department decided to fall back on its earlier plan of making do with labour from the goods sheds, and later in the day the staff of No. 3 goods shed was informed that they would have to go on the trucks. Once again refusal was immediate. The thirty casual labourers and six permanent men employed in the shed closed ranks and refused to 'usurp the places of the truckers' by acting as strike breakers.[29] Strong disciplinary action was instantly taken against them. The permanent hands were suspended and the casual hands dismissed, the latter in addition being advised that they would never again find employment with the Government.[30] This action may well have succeeded in making evident the Department's willingness to take severe measures in support of its policy. Yet, it was now in a worse position than before. It had no truckers, and no staff in No. 3 goods shed where there was always work to be attended to. To overcome the latter difficulty arrangements were made to set up a skeleton staff of ten permanent hands drawn from No. 1 goods shed, but they in turn refused 'to take the places of their mates'. Instant dismissal followed, it being held that 'discipline could not be maintained if such an action was tolerated'. The very act of disciplining these hands, however, provoked further trouble, for the 50 casual labourers in the shed immediately came out in sympathy.[31]

The significance of the numerous expressions of solidarity exhibited during these early days of the strike must not be overlooked. They are indicative of an emerging class consciousness and class sympathy, never previously witnessed on a similar scale. The lumpers, the truckers and the goods shed workers were coming to recognise the broader foundations on which their joint economic interests rested.

The discharged railway workers were quick to canvass political assistance. Within hours of their dismissal they laid their case before the representatives of the four Fremantle seats in the Legislative Assembly and convinced them that their grievance was genuine. The MLAs came out strongly in support of the strikers. They protested publicly 'against a Government department taking the side of the Steamship Owners Association' and took immediate steps to arrange a conference with F. Piesse, the Commissioner of Railways.[32]

At the conference held on the following day, 3rd March, the Government was repeatedly accused of conniving with private capital to lower wages. Piesse reiterated the official argument that the timing of events was merely coincidental and though the Parliamentarians threatened to censure him in the House for his 'moral error,' refused to revert to the arrangements in force before the strike.[33]

While the conference was in progress, the situation on the waterfront took a turn which put to the test the Railway Department's ability to implement its new proposals. Two steamers, the *Essex* and the *Karrakatta*, put into Fremantle with cargo to unload. The local agents, Strelitz Bros., were in sympathy with the lumpers and prepared to pay the old rates, hence no problems were anticipated. Moving the cargo from the wharf to the goods sheds, however, involved the use of truckers, and feelings ran high when it was learned that the Department intended to employ a makeshift gang drawn from the goods sheds and stations between Perth and Fremantle.[34] A large crowd which had assembled on the wharf gave the gang a rowdy reception when they arrived for work and it seemed that there would be a breach of the peace. None such occurred and the events which followed show how rapidly the unionists were developing a feel for industrial strategy. Realising that violence would only lead to police intervention and adverse publicity, they 'commenced to use their persuasive powers to induce the men not to blackleg ... on their fellow workers'. This move paid ample dividends, for so many were won over that operations on the wharf came to a halt. Simultaneously, the lumpers on board the two vessels concerned refused to work if non-unionist truckers were employed, and with this demonstration of unity produced a deadlock which forcefully underlined the emerging power of organised labour.

Undeterred by this early reverse the Department made two further attempts at using strike breakers in the trucks, but both ended in failure. On the first occasion persuasion again sufficed to win over the non-union men; on the second, the crowd intervened while the unionists were canvassing their case and prevented the new truckers from reaching the ships by uncoupling the railway wagons in which they were travelling. It appears that few unionists were involved in this show of force — 'not ten' according to one of their officials — and that it was the general public that took the law into its own hands.[35] That there was a considerable sympathy for the unionists in Fremantle is beyond question. In the early days of the strike there were reports of 'free labourers' being roughly handled in the town, and not always were unionists held to be responsible;[36] when the Railway Department introduced non-union labour into one of the goods sheds, a crowd of 'several hundreds,' not all of whom could possibly have been truckers, tried to break into the building;[37] and after the disturbances created by the townspeople on the dockside, one of the leading members of the Steamship Owners Association, W.E. Moxon, found that none of the town's cabbies were prepared to carry him.[38]

As the disaffection in Fremantle grew, the town's electoral representatives stepped up their efforts on the truckers' behalf with a hard hitting letter to the Premier, Sir John Forrest. Repeating the charge of collusion and justifying the demand for retaining the existing wage, they called upon him to intervene on the side of the truckers.[39] The dimensions of the strike also continued to grow. Truckers in Albany and Geraldton stopped work, and in Fremantle the staff of goods shed No. 4, though not required to change their normal routine, came out in sympathy with their colleagues.[40]

With the public, the politicians and the truckers lined up against him, the Commissioner of Railways realised that his 'hard line' policy had little chance of success. The lumpers' strike did not involve the Government, but the truckers' issue did, and it was clearly in Forrest's political interest to prevent a further escalation in criticism of his administration. Rather than wait for the inevitable directive from the Premier, the Commissioner announced that he had reconsidered the question and that in order to counter the charge of collusion, the new conditions under which the truckers were to be employed were postponed for two months, and all those suspended as a result of the incidents of the previous week were to be immediately reinstated.[41]

That these concessions were considerable is beyond question. Yet there was little hope of their settling the issues at stake, particularly if non-union labour were to be employed on the wharves in the near future. The lumpers magnanimously proposed that their dispute be treated as a quite separate issue and urged the truckers to resume work,[42] but the very next day — 6 March — events on the waterside showed that such a separation was not feasible and that both disputes had necessarily to be settled together.

On that morning two ships owned by companies in the Steamship Owners Association, the *Wollowra* and the *Adelaide*, prepared to unload cargo. Both intended to use 'free labour' and the former had on board 'labourers specially brought over from Adelaide for the purpose.' The truckers at first manned the trucks, but their loyalties proved too strong and to the delight of a large and rather hostile crowd which had gathered to watch the proceedings, they soon refused to continue working.[43] Piesse was infuriated by the turn of events. Believing that the public no longer had justifiable grounds for criticism, he dismissed the entire body of truckers and began to recruit free labour. When an adequate number of the latter could not be found, railway employees from elsewhere were ordered to Fremantle, but the majority refused to work, preferring suspension to blacklegging on the colleagues. Further attempts to gather labour from other sections of the Department led to more dismissals, and though a few men agreed to work, the total pool of truckers remained woefully short until the strike finally ended.[44]

The truckers' refusal to dissociate themselves from the lumpers' strike had a considerable impact on the Steamship Owners Association. The Association had assumed that the lumpers' resistance to the new regulations would be short-lived if its ships 'were hung up for a fortnight.'[45] When the incidents of the 6th made it clear that the struggle could last somewhat longer, the Association adopted a stronger attitude. Pointing out that it controlled two-thirds of the shipping in the port, that its financial resources were far superior to those of the Union, and that it had fought and defeated 'the whole strength of the labour organisations from Queensland to Victoria' over a period of thirteen weeks, a spokesman warned that the Association would not give in 'even if the fight lasted for twelve months.'[46]

Merchants with perishable cargoes on the struck ships now began to grow anxious over the fate of their goods and a meeting with representatives of the Unions was arranged to work out ways and means of releasing specified types of cargo. The Union responded most sympathetically. The secretary, with an eye no doubt on the goodwill the Union could earn, expressed his willingness to request the lumpers not only to land the goods but to load them onto the trucks as well. However, he was doubtful as to whether the companies concerned would allow the lumpers to board their ships.

The secretary proved to be right. The agents were so intent on crushing the lumpers that they were unwilling to permit work of any description, except on the new terms laid down by the Association. The merchants were accordingly fobbed off with the unconvincing argument that their suggestion was unfeasible since perishable goods were not stored together but 'were mixed up with other lines of merchandise.'[47]

That this reaction was a tactical blunder was immediately apparent. The merchants berated the shipping companies in the strongest terms, contrasting the latter's behaviour with the sympathy shown by the lumpers. Expressions of displeasure were also forthcoming from a number of other sources. The *West Australian* commented editorially that unionism was 'too deeply rooted in Australia to be eradicated, yet the Association feels itself strong enough to declare against it;' five parliamentary representatives of the Fremantle district 'gave their cordial support to the Lumpers Union', and even the Salvation Army declared that its members would not 'take passage by any of the steamers owned by the Steamship Owners Association.'[48]

Up to this point the attitude of the public does not appear to have concerned the Association. Working class support for the lumpers they had chosen to ignore, but the merchants, the press and the Salvation Army were another matter. On 7th March, the Association put its case to the public for the first time. It argued that the wages ruling in the port before 1st March had been set at a time when labour was short and that rates had now been brought down to a 'more normal level.' Moreover, the new rates were not only somewhat higher than those current in the pre-1896 period, they also represented an increase in real wages as the cost of living had declined since then. Regarding freedom of contract in the docks the ship owners reiterated their earlier stand, justifying it on the grounds that a closed shop would 'in many instances seriously interfere with the satisfactory working of their business.'[49]

Though the Association's statement had little impact on the views of most of its critics, it succeeded in tempering the attitude of the press. The latter now began to argue that there was something to be said for both sides, and to urge the setting up of some form of conciliatory machinery.[50] The suggestion was quickly taken up by the Mayor of Fremantle, J. McHenry Clark, and the MLA for Fremantle, J.J. Higham. Neither of the disputants showed any great enthusiasm for the idea, but to refuse participation would have been fatal to their respective public images, and on the eighth morning representatives from each side met in conference under the chairmanship of the Mayor. After some initial skirmishing there emerged a surprising mutual willingness to make concessions on a number of issues, *e.g.*, the employers were prepared to consider reverting to the old rates for day labour and the men to consider acceptance of a lowering of the old scale for overtime; again, the employers were prepared to pay for the greater part of the time taken in going out to ships anchored in the roads, and the men to accept payment for one way only. On the all important question of freedom of contract, however, no agreement could be reached and this became the issue on which the conference foundered. The Association insisted that 'the master must have the free right to deal with his men exactly as he wishes to,' and the Union just as resolutely declared that freedom of contract should not be permitted. Considering the progress made in other directions the chairman proposed that a small committee chosen from both parties should have further discussions on the matter, but the Association was only prepared to deal with the lumpers as individuals and not as representatives of a Union. The implication here was that the employers were not prepared to recognise the existence of the Union and this introduced a new and serious issue into the dispute. The lumpers would have none of it and as it was evident that further discussion was purposeless, the conference came to an end.[51]

Neither the Union nor the Association showed any concern over the failure of these initial negotiations. The shipowners, convinced that victory would ultimately be theirs, were prepared to bide their time, while the lumpers believed that the best strategy was 'to let things take their course.' Work by a handful of locally recruited non-unionists was so slow and inefficient that it was bound to hurt the Association. Said a Union spokesman: "The present rate of discharge will cripple them. Someone has to pay for the detention of the ships, the breakage of cargo, and the slow delivery."[52]

If prolongation of the strike was expected to have an adverse impact on the incomes of the shipowners, there was no doubt whatever that the lumpers would earn nothing over the same period. The Trades and Labour Council opened a subscription list on the Union's behalf and called on the public for financial support. The response was immediate. The dock workers were an important part of Fremantle's economy and a cessation of spending on their part threatened dire economic results. Within a matter of days a stream of funds poured in from contributors in every walk of life. Traders, hoteliers, bakers, shopowners, bootmakers, butchers, tobacconists, cabbies, a variety of unions and even a prominent MLA rallied to the TLC's call. Considerable sums were also said to have been paid in directly to the TLC by kindred societies in Western Australia and the adjoining colonies, and with these resources at its disposal, the Lumpers Union was able to make an adequate strike allowance to its members.[53]

Apart from helping to finance the lumpers the TLC also attempted to use the strike to publicise a demand for compulsory arbitration. Problems of the order then faced by the community would not arise, it was held, if a Compulsory Arbitration Act, on the lines of that current in New Zealand, was to be introduced immediately.[54] Interestingly, the lumpers did not rush to support the proposal. The flood of contributions from the public appears to have convinced them that they would be able to hold out until the disruption in the port had crippled the shipowners and forced them to give in.

The optimism and complacency of the unionists was rudely shattered on the very next day when the *Bothwell Castle* put in from Adelaide with a number of 'free' labourers on board.[55] The importation of free labour was not new, for in the previous week the *Wollowra* had carried eleven 'free' truckers as part of her crew. On that occasion, however, the unionists had won them over in a matter of hours and their presence had no influence on the course of the strike. Circumstances were different now. The Government had closed off the jetty after the incidents connected with the *Adelaide* and the *Wollowra*, and the lumpers could no longer use their powers of persuasion. The Union was quick to allege collusion and the charge appears to have had some foundation, the more so since passes to enter the jetty were issued by the steamship companies and not by the Government. Nevertheless, no concessions were allowed and as a result the *Bothwell Castle* was able to discharge its cargo unimpeded and so raise the total discharge rate in the port to quite respectable proportions.[56] The implications of this sequence of events was not lost upon the Union and brought an immediate change in tactics. It was evident that what had been done once could be done again and that the time had come to abandon its earlier stand and press for a quick settlement.

Just at this juncture the editor of the *West Australian*, A. Lovekin, wrote to the disputants suggesting that the strike be referred to an arbitration board elected by both sides, and that the decision of the board be accepted as final. Compulsory arbitration had been mooted by the Trades and Labour Council when the strike was barely one week old, and now that their fortunes had changed for the worse the lumpers seized upon Lovekin's proposal. But not so the Association. Recognising the vulnerability of the Union, it argued that conditions had altered since the conference organised by the Mayor of Fremantle, and that it could no longer offer what had been offered then. Discussions would have to be *de novo* and, moreover, could only take place if the lumpers first agreed to concede that there would henceforth be 'freedom of contract' on the waterside.[57]

This *volte face* on the part of the Association, and its insistence that as a pre-requisite to further discussion the lumpers should concede what had become the main issue at stake in the strike, threw the Union into complete disarray. Until then orderliness had been a characteristic of the lumpers' behaviour and had been favourably remarked upon time and time again by the press.[58] On the afternoon of 15th March this self-discipline was abandoned. The lumpers appear to have decided that a show of strength would do more to advance their cause. Taking the police by surprise, they charged the jetty, took possession of the ships berthed alongside, and cleared every free labourer out of the port. Between 40 and 50 free labourers were hunted off four ships by some 300 to 400 men, cheered on by a huge crowd of townspeople who had gathered to watch. There were some cases of assault, but these were fewer than one might have expected, both because the ships' companies sympathised with the strikers and made no attempt to prevent them coming aboard, and because some Union leaders intervened personally to prevent violence and destruction of property.[59]

That the lumpers had committed a major tactical error in resorting to force was quickly evident, for it made infinitely worse the very handicaps against which they were protesting. Indeed, the Union guaranteed this result by issuing a rather belligerent statement within hours of the incident. Charging the authorities with taking sides by closing off the jetty and so preventing unionists from reasoning with the free labourers, the lumpers' president declared that if the Government did '... not concede ... the right which we claim, to reason with these men, we will have to force the position. We have commenced and we intend to follow it up, no matter what the result may be.'[60]

This threat fuelled the uproar created by the earlier events of the day. The steamship owners called upon the Government to step in and prevent a 'repetition of such lawless proceedings as those of today at Fremantle,'[61] and the Government was not slow to respond. A number of unionists were arrested, the police guard on the jetty was increased to between 50 and 60 officers and police protection was offered to all free labourers who sought it.[62] The press added its voice, maintaining that the principal issue now was one of law and order, and went on to predict that the strikers had so damaged their cause that the disturbances on the waterfront would prove 'a prelude to the collapse of the strike.'[63]

Neither the stern measures taken by the Government nor the prognostications of the press deterred the Union from pursuing its declared aim of 'forcing the position.' The next morning it called out *all* union labour connected with shipping, irrespective of whether the companies affected were members of the Association or not. Simultaneously, steps were taken to persuade the entire body of railway employees in the port to come out in sympathy.[64] The dispute had reached a critical stage. If the engine drivers struck and the trains on the waterfront stopped running, the movement of cargoes from shipside to goods shed and *vice versa* would have come to a halt, and the Association's use of non-union labour would have been most effectively countered. The lumpers could then have sat back and waited until impending bankruptcy forced the Association to surrender. But the engine drivers, though sympathetic to the Union's cause and willing to extend financial support, refused to come out on strike.[65] Their decision proved of crucial importance. To the steamship owners it brought the scent of victory. The *Marloo* had docked that very morning with a gang of free labourers on board, and more were on the water en route from Adelaide.[66] Confronted thus with the threat of redundancy, it seemed unlikely that the lumpers would resist much longer. Having restarted work in the port with their skeleton force of non-union labour, all of whom were now billeted on a collier owned by the Adelaide Steamship Company and so out of the Union's reach, the Association expectantly awaited the inevitable collapse of the strike.[67]

To the unionists the decision brought a sense of despair. With access to the heavily guarded jetty denied them, with an increasing stream of non-union labour being shipped in to join the men already at work, and with operations in the port slowly getting under way again, the prospect of defeat seemed perilously close. In the circumstances it seemed foolish to jeopardise the goodwill of those shipowners with whom the Union had no quarrel. On 20th March the resolution that work on all ships should cease was rescinded and unionists went back to work on neutral vessels.[68]

Ironically, it was over the unloading of a neutral vessel that matters in the port finally came to a head. The German ship *Karlsruhe*, whose local agents, Diamond, Son and Saurmann, had held aloof from the move to reduce wages, docked on the 24th to unload cargo and take on 300 tons of coal. It was over the question of providing bunkers that a major issue developed, for the only secure source of coal supply in Fremantle was the Adelaide Steamship Company whose hulks were crewed solely be free labourers. When it was announced that both loading and unloading were to proceed simultaneously, the lumpers refused to work without police protection on the grounds that they would be outnumbered three to one by the free labourers, some of whom harboured bitter feelings towards the Union. The request for police protection, however, was dismissed as 'specious,' and the agents, seeing that the lumpers would not work without it, declared that they had no alternative but to employ free labour.[69] This decision greatly irked the lumpers. Their indignation was further heightened by the arrival of the *Kalgoorlie* with more non-union labour aboard, and by the information that the *New Guinea* would put in the next morning with yet another contingent.[70]

Anticipating trouble the police made elaborate arrangements on the 25th morning to ensure that work on the *Karlsruhe* was not interfered with. All other shipping operations in the port were suspended so as to ensure that every available constable was at hand to protect the German vessel. As a result, a force of 56 officers, later augmented to 70, was assembled and stationed in a cordon which kept the wharf clear from one end of the steamer to the other. Work began at 10 a.m. in the presence of a small crowd of onlookers and for some hours proceeded without incident. At 12.30 p.m. the unionists marched down from the town in a body, but made no attempt to breach the police cordon. All that they asked was that two representatives should be allowed on board 'to confer peaceably with the free labourers and endeavour to persuade them to come out.'[71]

After some discussion between the ship's captain, the agents and the police, the unionists' request was granted and at 2 p.m. their representatives sat down to a conference with two delegates elected by the free labourers. As the conference proceeded it became apparent that the free labourers were not to be easily won over. More that half their number had been shipped in from the eastern colonies and were not as amenable to persuasion as the earlier local recruits had been. This was soon sensed by the main body of lumpers out on the wharf. Thus far they had behaved reasonably well, their protests being limited to some hooting, the occasional catcall, and on one occasion to the throwing of a few stones by a single individual. But as the afternoon wore on their patience and self-control came to an end. Backed up by the crowd, which by now had swelled to considerable proportions, the lumpers rushed the police lines and tried to get through to the ship. Force was met by force. The police used their batons with telling effect, stones were thrown, blows were exchanged and blood flowed freely. The captain of the *Karlsruhe* brought a melodramatic touch to the events of the day, '... standing at the gangway of his vessel with a loaded revolver, ... threatening to shoot any invader, while the crew were armed with marling spikes, pieces of old iron, and other weapons.'[72]

Despite their numerical superiority the lumpers were no match for the organised forces ranged against them. A number were arrested and the wharf was eventually cleared and sealed off. In addition, their representatives at the conference were unable to extract the merest concession from the free labourers on board and it appeared that the union had been routed.[73]

Yet, in another sense the exercise brought a resounding victory. The captain of the *Karlsruhe* decided that operations in Fremantle were attended by too many risks and the next morning sailed for the eastern colonies with the bulk of his cargo undischarged and his bunkers less than half full.[74] The implications were not lost upon the Government and the Association: despite the precautions they had taken there were still occasions when disruptive action could succeed. What was just as alarming was the lack of strong public feeling against the course adopted by the Union. Indeed, public sympathy appeared to have increased. An open air concert held in aid of the strikers on the night following the clash 'was packed right to the entrance' and netted over £40, while two days later donations to the strike fund reached the record weekly total of £97. 5s.[75] With financial support of that order behind them there was the likelihood that the lumpers could be encouraged to continue with their strong-arm tactics until economic considerations forced the Association to submit to their demands.

The elaborate preparations subsequently made to frustrate any such intention suggest collaboration between the Government and the Association. At a special meeting of the Cabinet on 27 March it was decided that in the interests of law and order, free labourers wishing to work on the waterfront would receive 'such protection as would enable them successfully to do so.' In other words it was not believed that the preservation of law and order required any concessions from the Association; it was made synonymous with the maintenance of the Association's stand on freedom of contract. In order to provide this protection, the Police Commissioner was instructed to increase the force on duty in the port, and in a matter of hours the strength of the police contingent was raised to one hundred men. In addition, the steps earlier taken to prevent all contact between the Union and free labourers billeted on the ships in port were continued, with entry to the docks requiring a pass issued by the companies concerned or by the Minister for Railways.

The Cabinet was also perturbed by the readiness with which the public assembled in large crowds to support the lumpers at the slightest hint of a confrontation. To discourage the practice they now warned that if there was a recurrence of 'riotous behaviour' severe measures would have to be taken, not only 'with the men ... directly offending, but also with those ... associated with them in large bodies,' for 'those who assemble with the actual offenders must take the responsibility of their act in being present.' The Commissioner of Police revealed the difference between the 'severe measures' envisaged and those resorted to in previous disturbances, when he declared that 'in the event of the police having to resort to the use of their firearms the public would be consulting their own welfare by keeping away from the crowd.'[76]

In the face of these new restrictions the lumpers had the good sense to abandon all thought of further disruptive action. Financially, the Union was healthy enough, for apart from public subscriptions a 'large amount of financial support' was now coming in from the goldfields' unions.[77] But this financial assistance would not continue indefinitely. If defeat was to be avoided a new strategy had to be evolved without delay, and in what appears to have been a last desperate move, the lumpers once again advocated the principle of compulsory arbitration. This was the only feasible option left open to the union and fortunately there were influential sections of the public willing to act immediately on the proposal. The parliamentary representatives of the Fremantle area promptly took the question up with the employers and urged that the dispute be referred to a board consisting of three nominees from each side with a judge of the Supreme Court as referee.[78]

The Association did not favour the idea. The new arrangements in the port had so circumscribed the Union that there was every reason to expect an unconditional surrender of the strikers. Nevertheless, as it would have been impolitic to refuse, the employers agreed to participate, though on terms which they knew the lumpers could not possible accept. They insisted once again that discussions could only take place if 'freedom of contract was absolutely ceded and left outside the issue,' and demanded also that Mr. Rasmussen, the secretary of the Union, be excluded from the talks, 'as he was not an employee of any of the steamship companies.' This intractable attitude sufficed to deter the Fremantle MLAs from persisting with their proposal, but not so other sections of the community. Merchants whose businesses had suffered from the stoppage, church dignitaries alarmed by the prospect of more violence, parliamentarians in Perth sympathetic to labour, and a miscellaneous collection of others prominent in community affairs, met under the chairmanship of the city's Mayor, Alexander Forrest, to explore the possibility of bringing the two sides to the conference table. Anticipating the terms earlier advanced by the Association, the meeting resolved that further talks, implicitly without preconditions, should be held, and that each party should have the freedom to choose their own representatives. A citizens' committee made up of the Mayor of Perth, the Anglican Bishop Rev. Riley, the Catholic Bishop Rev. Gibney, the Rev. G. Rowe, Chairman of the Methodist Church, A. Lovekin of the *West Australian,* J. Rae of Foy and Gibsons, and T. Cockburn of Bon Marche, was then elected to convey these resolutions to the disputants.[79]

When communicating with the two sides the Committee sought to mediate, not arbitrate, and to do so in such a fashion as to arrive at a viable 'basis for conference.' Their approach proved eminently successful. After discussions with both parties the issues at stake were put into a number of categories and it was agreed that these should be dealt with at a conference.[80] To the lumpers even this initial step was something of a triumph, for influenced perhaps by the composition of the committee, the Association did not think it prudent to persist with its earlier objections or even to challenge Rasmussen's presence as a union representative.[81]

The conference met on 3rd April, and a number of thorny issues were resolved with surprising ease. Where freedom of contract was concerned, the Union conceded to the shipowners the right to employ whom they pleased and to conduct their business in their own way. The shipowners in turn gave the assurance that they would not object to any or all of the men employed by them being members of the Union. The Union also conceded the right of the shipowners to engage as many men as the stevedore thought necessary, and the employers agreed that if the sufficiency of that number was disputed the matter should be settled by calling in an independent stevedore. On the question of men sent out to Gage Roads,

Owen Anchorage, Rockingham, etc. not being paid until they actually started work, the Association agreed that they would in future pay for the time spent in getting there, though not for the return journey.

On the two major issues of wages and hours of work, however, agreement could not be reached. The lumpers were prepared to submit the points in dispute to arbitration, but the shipowners were at first unwilling to concede the principle. After repeated interviews and under pressure from the Committee they ultimately gave way 'as a matter of expediency on the present occasion to accept the opinion of judges.' The *modus operandi* decided upon was that each side should choose an arbitrator and that the arbitrators in turn should appoint an umpire who would vote in the event of a deadlock. The lumpers nominated the Reverend Rowe, the employers picked Bishop Gibney, and the arbitrators then chose Bishop Riley as umpire.

After two hours deliberation and much consultation the arbitrators announced their award. It was held that during the week the working day was to fall between 8 a.m. and 6 p.m., eight hours of which were to be paid for at the ordinary rate. On Saturdays the working day was to extend from 8 a.m. to 1 p.m. with all labour performed outside these times being classed as 'overtime.' The award represented a considerable improvement upon the hours which the shipping companies had sought to introduce in March, since it lengthened the previous working day by only one hour and not three.

The wage rates awarded fell into a number of categories, *i.e.*, *General cargo*: Day work, 1s. 1-½d. an hour; overtime, 1s. 8d.; Sundays and holidays, 2s. 6d. all through. *Coal:* Day work, 1s. 3d. an hour; overtime, 2s.; Sundays and holidays, 2s. 6d. all through; with all rates to remain in force for at least 12 months. The day and overtime rates awarded for general cargo were similar to those announced by the owners in March and thus represented a reduction in the lumpers' existing wage scale. The 2s. 6d. payable for Sunday and holiday work was 3d. above that offered by the Association, but in reality the men lost here as well since prior to the strike 2s. 6d. had been allowed for holidays and 4s. for Sundays. In the case of coaling the award favoured the Union. The employers' decision to substitute a daily rate with payment by 'tonnage loaded per day' was set aside, and the wage scale in force prior to the strike retained, though here as well the Sunday rate of 4s. was lowered to a flat 2s. 6d. for Sundays and holidays.[82]

When the award was announced to the Union some 'rather warm opinions' were expressed, but the members ultimately abided by their undertaking to accept the decision of the arbitrators.[83] In any event there was little else they could do. Arbitration was the only option left to the Union, and they were fortunate indeed to have even that. With the lumpers' ratification of the terms of agreement the strike came to an end. On 5 April, after exactly five weeks, the unionists returned to work on the vessels of the Steamship Owners Association.

All things considered it might seem that the Association came off somewhat better then the Union. The shipowners retained the right to employ whom they pleased and to conduct their business as they wished. In other words, there was to be as much 'freedom of contract' on the wharf after the strike as there had been before it. Moreover, the rates agreed upon for working general cargo were virtually those proposed by the Association, and the bulk of the goods cleared through Fremantle fell within that category. Nonetheless, the gains made by the Union should not be underplayed. Rasmussen's presence at the conference and the willingness of the employers to hold talks with official Union delegates implied a recognition of the Union; the fact that the two sides negotiated the future terms of employment signified an acceptance of the principle of collective bargaining; and that such important issues as those concerning wages and hours of work should be decided by independent mediators amounted to an acceptance of the Union's demand for arbitration. When one adds to this the improved rates for coaling, and the payments made for time expended in travelling to ships not berthed alongside, it becomes evident that the advantages won by the men were not inconsiderable.

The agreement reached at the conference also brought about a final settlement of the truckers' dispute. The shipowners agreed not to differentiate between lumpers and truckers and the latter's wages were brought in line with the arbitrators' award. It will be recalled that after an attempt at wage-cutting the Railway Department had been forced to revert temporarily to pre-strike wage levels. Hence the new arrangements brought two scales into being, one paid by the Government and the other by the shipping companies. The Government now brought rates down to the conference levels, but as these were higher than those originally proposed in the declaration of 15th February, the truckers lost less than they otherwise might have.[84]

All went well on the waterfront in the days immediately following the end of the strike. The free labourers obtained in the colony were reported to be 'clearing out from the shipping in numbers,' and the imported hands to be prepared 'to take their departure eastwards by early boats.'[85] Prosecutions by the police of those involved in the disturbances on the wharf were dropped and it was generally believed that the situation in the port was rapidly reverting to normal.[86] Yet, a week had barely elapsed before it became evident that the dispute was by no means over. On the 11th the *Willyama,* a steamer belonging to the Adelaide Steamship Company, put in to discharge coal, and the lumpers' suspicions were aroused when a police guard was stationed around the vessel with instructions that members of the Union should be prevented from going on board. Inquiries revealed that a gang of 'imported' free labourers had been engaged on a 48 hour contract to discharge coal for a sum of 48s. each, *i.e.*, at 1s. an hour. As this was below the 1s. 3d. decided upon by the arbitrators, the Union immediately charged the Company with being in violation of the conference agreement. The local manager of the Company tried at first to absolve his firm from criticism by arguing that though the boat was indeed owned by the Adelaide Steamship Company it was chartered by an 'outside stevedore,' consequently the Company had nothing to do with the rates of pay. The next day a little probing revealed that the *Willyama* was on charter to the Labour Bureau, an agency set up by the Association to recruit free labourers during the strike.[87] This showed that not only the Adelaide Steamship Company but the other members of the Association as well were parties to a scheme which sought to circumvent the one major decision of the arbitrators on the question of wages which had gone in favour of the men. Realising that they had been found out the shipowners shifted their ground and advanced a new argument in justification of the arrangement. It was contended that the rates agreed upon at the conference covered only casual labour, whereas the men working on the *Willyama* were permanently employed. It is true that permanent engagements were not considered at the conference, and that all dock labour in Fremantle was casual. Nonetheless, the argument was patently absurd, for as the *West Australian* put it, 'to contend that a forty-eight hours' engagement constitutes a permanent contract of employment surely offends the commonsense of men.'[88]

Alarmed that the defiant attitude of the shipowners would precipitate a renewal of the strike, the business community proposed that the Citizens' committee be called on again to act as mediators.[89] The suggestion won early support from the Union. The latter initially hinted at the possibility of strong acticn which would take 'others' out with them, but considering the ability of the Association to import labour, and the willingness of the Government to provide that labour with police protection, this was obviously a tactic to be avoided until all else had failed.[90]

The employers had no reason to favour yet another meeting, but within the space of a week a number of incidents prompted a change of stance and brought them to the conference table. On 14th April a critical leader in the *West Australian* charged that 'the new ground of offence comes from the Owners Association,' and assured the Union that 'both the temper and influence of the community' were such as to uphold 'the distinction between fair play and the reverse.'[91] Two days later the Shipowners Association of Melbourne telegraphed Premier Forrest promising support for the recent agreement 'in both spirit and letter,' and announced their intention of holding an inquiry into the new crisis.[92] On 19th April a number of free labourers employed by the Adelaide Steamship Company greatly embarrassed the Company by revealing that they had been coaxed into staying on after the strike 'with a bit of beer and tobacco'; those who wanted passages back to the east had been put off 'without any reason,' and the Company, they claimed, was now attempting to retain their services by holding wages in arrear.[93] Worse still, a few of those so treated sued the Company on 21st April and judgment was given in favour of the plaintiffs, with costs.[94] Finally, the lumpers, realising that the Company would be obliged to tread carefully because of the manner in which these several events had undermined its credibility, switched to an unexpectedly militant policy. Between 14th and 19th April they exercised their 'freedom of contract' by refusing to work three of the Association's vessels, and on 20 April both lumpers and truckers ceased work on all shipping in the port.[95] This succession of misfortunes persuaded the Association that aggressive tactics would be ill-suited to the times, and on the evening of the 20th it agreed to meet the Union for a second round of discussions.[96]

The conference sat on 24th April and deliberated for three days. On this occasion there was no arbitration; the committee merely served as mediators striving for the best settlement possible under existing circumstances and each side made concessions in the interests of industrial harmony. The Union conceded that the Association had the right to contract for any of their work with whomsoever they chose, and the shipowners agreed that when such contracts were let, payment would be at the rates earlier accepted by the Union, *i.e.*, 1s. 3d. an hour ordinary time, 2s. an hour overtime and 2s. 5d. for Sundays and holidays.[97] The agreement brought peace with honour to both sides. It preserved the freedom of contract on which the Association had consistently insisted, and prevented the wage cutting which the Union regarded as the inevitable consequence of such freedom. Thereafter the situation on the waterfront returned to a state of amity which was not to be seriously disturbed until 1917. Of the fate of the free labourers little is known, but as no further disputes over their employment are recorded one can only assume that the imported hands returned to the eastern colonies, and that those recruited locally were peaceably absorbed by the Union.

Viewed in retrospect the most interesting feature of the strike is the manner in which its participants and their supporters conducted themselves. One is struck by the sense of solidarity which permeated the Union and led its members to stand fast at a time when high unemployment might have been expected to tempt some to forgo principle for security. No less remarkable is the fashion in which the working class in general rallied behind the Union. The refusal of the overwhelming majority of the unemployed to act as strike-breakers — which made it necessary for the Association to import hands from the eastern colonies, and the willingness of fellow unionists to subscribe generously to the strike fund — which permitted the lumpers to stay out for five weeks, reflects the growing maturity of organised labour. Never before had action of this sort been attempted or even suggested by workers in Western Australia. Admittedly, much had yet to be learned in the tactical sphere. Had the engine drivers refused to work instead of merely extending financial aid the strike might have terminated earlier and with a more favourable sequel for the lumpers, and a similar result would probably have eventuated had the T.L.C. brought its member unions out in sympathy.

To the shipowners the strike was a revealing experience. In its initial stages they were contemptuous of the Union, as well they might be after the resounding manner in which labour organisations had been defeated all over Australia in the early 1890s. As the strike progressed and it was found that a sufficiency of strike-breakers could not be recruited locally, and as labour in general began to close ranks behind the lumpers, the employers came to realise that times had changed. Their subsequent willingness to bargain with the Union and the tacit recognition that this implied, mark out the five weeks of the strike as a period of transition in the Association's attitude to labour. Given the importance of the shipping interests in Western Australia, and the publicity which accompanied every stage of the strike, this change in stance had implications for the entire body of employers in the colony. It is no accident that thereafter a new respect for labour is to be discerned in the relationship between master and man.

The strike played a similar catalytic role in the Government's approach to industrial relations. The official hostility towards the Union, which led the Railway Department to collaborate with the shipowners and the police to protect their interests on the waterfront, brought the Government so close to the dispute that it was able to observe at close quarters the gradual transformation in the tactics and views of both Association and Union. The success of conciliation and arbitration in settling so speedily an issue which had disrupted the community for five weeks confirmed the impression that a qualitative change was occurring in the sphere of labour relations. The Government had not previously been well disposed to the principle of arbitration. In fact, Premier Sir John Forrest had categorically refused to entertain the idea when it was repeatedly suggested by the Trades and Labour Council prior to 1899. Now, so eminently suited did it seem to the context that was emerging in Western Australia, that a prejudice developed in its favour. Within the space of a year a compulsory Conciliation and Arbitration Act was on the statute book, and the principle rapidly became the pivot on which the entire industrial relations system turned.

As pointed out in an earlier essay the immediate reasons for this change sprang from Forrest's desire to be in office when Federation of the Australian colonies was achieved, but the peaceful resolution of the dispute on the docks must have contributed to the Premier's shift of stance by demonstrating to him the advantages of arbitration over strong industrial action.

The impact of the lumpers' strike upon worker, employer and Government, the attitudinal changes that it engendered, and its influence on future developments in the industrial field, gives it a special significance which justifies the claim that it was a bench-mark in Western Australian labour history.

REFERENCES

1. T.A. Coghlan, *Labour and Industry in Australia*, Oxford, 1918, 2081-82.
2. V. Ashworth, 'A History of the Fremantle Lumpers Union 1889-1919,' Unpublished essay, W.A. Archives. HS/PR 1890.
3. Coghlan, *op. cit.*, 2076.
4. *Ibid.*, 2173.
5. *The West Australian* (hereafter WA), 16-11-96.
6. The minute books of the Lumpers Union and of the Steamship Owners Association for 1899 are no longer extant. The numerous references made to the *West Australian* should not however be taken to mean that this study is almost wholly dependent on the impressions of newspaper reporters. It was the practice of the *West Australia* to report the proceedings of meetings of both Union and Association, and to publish in full such statements as were made by office-bearers of both bodies during the course of the strike.
7. Coghlan, *op. cit.*, 2070.
8. *W.A.*, 13-3-99.
9. *W.A.*, 4-3-99.
10. *W.A.* and *The Morning Herald* (hereafter MH), 16-2-99.
11. *W.A.*, 17-2-99.
12. *M.H.*, 16-2-99.
13. *W.A.*, 16-2-99. Some days later a member of the Association justified the reductions by referring to the 'existing circumstances of trade', but made no attempt to support his opinion with facts and figures. *W.A.*, 12-2-99.
14. *W.A.*, 17-2-99.
15. *Ibid.*
16. *W.A.* and *M.H.*, 20-2-99.
17. *Ibid.*
18. *W.A.*, 21-2-99.
19. *M.H.* and *W.A.*, 21-2-99.
20. *W.A.*, 22-2-99.
21. *W.A.*, 23-2-99.
22. *W.A.*, 27-2-99 and 6-3-99.
23. *W.A.*, 2-3-99.
24. *W.A.*, 27-2-99 and 2-3-99.
25. This is an aspect of the lumpers dispute which has been greatly neglected. Ashworth alone treats it in any detail.

26. *W.A.*, 2 and 4-3-99.
27. *W.A.*, 2-3-99.
28. *W.A.*, 3-3-99 and 4-3-99.
29. *W.A.* and *M.H.*, 2-3-99.
30. *W.A.*, 3-3-99 and 4-3-99.
31. *W.A.*, 3-3-99.
32. *W.A.*, and *M.H.*, 3-3-99.
33. *W.A.*, 4-3-99.
34. *Ibid.*
35. *W.A.*, 6-3-99.
36. *W.A.*, 3-3-99 and 4-3-99.
37. *W.A.*, 6-3-99.
38. *Ibid.*
39. *Ibid.*
40. *W.A.*, 4-3-99 and 6-3-99.
41. *W.A.*, 6-3-99 and 7-3-99.
42. *W.A.*, 6-3-99.
43. *W.A.*, 7-3-99.
44. *W.A.*, 7-3-99 and 8-3-99.
45. *W.A.*, 4-3-99.
46. *W.A.*, 7-3-99.
47. *Ibid.*
48. *Ibid.*
49. *Ibid.*
50. *W.A.*, 6-3-99 and 8-3-99.
51. *W.A.*, 8-3-99, 9-3-99 and 10-3-99.
52. *W.A.*, 11-3-99.
53. *W.A.*, 9-3-99, 13-3-99 and 18-3-99.
54. *W.A.*, 8-3-99, 10-3-99 and 13-3-99.
55. *W.A.*, 13-3-99 and 14-3-99.
56. *W.A.*, 6-3-99, 8-3-99, 10-3-99 and 13-3-99.
57. *W.A.*, 14-3-99 and 16-3-99.
58. *W.A.*, 4-3-99 and 8-3-99.
59. *W.A.*, 16-3-99.
60. *Ibid.*
61. *Ibid.*
62. *Ibid.*
63. *Ibid.*
64. *W.A.*, 16-3-99 and 17-3-99.

65. *W.A.*, 18-3-99.
66. *Ibid.*
67. *W.A.*, 20-3-99.
68. *W.A.*, 21-3-99.
69. *W.A.*, 22-3-99.
70. *W.A.*, 23-3-99 and 24-3-99.
71. *W.A.*, 27-3-99.
72. *Ibid.*
73. *Ibid.*
74. *Ibid.*
75. *W.A.*, 30-3-99 and 1-4-99.
76. *W.A.*, 28-3-99.
77. *W.A.*, 6-4-99.
78. *W.A.*, 29-3-99 and 30-3-99.
79. *W.A.*, 30-3-99.
80. *W.A.*, 31-3-99 and 3-4-99.
81. *W.A.*, 3-4-99.
82. *W.A.*, 5-4-99
83. *Ibid.*
84. *W.A.*, 6-4-99 and 10-4-99.
85. *W.A.*, 5-4-99 and 6-4-99.
86. *W.A.*, 5-4-99.
87. *W.A.*, 12-4-99, 13-4-99, 14-4-99 and 15-4-99.
88. *W.A.*, 14-4-99 and 15-4-99.
89. *W.A.*, 13-4-99 and 14-4-99.
90. *W.A.*, 15-4-99.
91. *W.A.*, 14-4-99.
92. *W.A.*, 17-4-99.
93. *W.A.*, 22-4-99.
94. *W.A.*, 20-4-99 and 22-4-99.
95. *W.A.*, 19-2-99 and 21-2-99.
96. *W.A.*, 21-4-99.
97. *W.A.*, 27-4-99 and 1-5-99.

3

Master and Servant Laws in Western Australia*

Early Experiments in Master and Servant Legislation

The Master and Servant laws, which appeared at different times in the Australian colonies prior to Federation, were derived from precedents in medieval England. They supplied the terms of employment by defining the rights and obligations of labour and gave both workers and employers the right to summary hearings before magistrates, whenever disputes arose. The laws were enacted in different forms in the several colonies and were framed to cope with prevailing local conditions. As these varied from colony to colony, the Master and Servant laws, despite their common origin, were never a single body of law. In some cases emphasis was placed on the coercion of plantation labour, in others on the control of industrial workers and in others again, on the management of shepherds and herders.

In Western Australia, where settlement began in 1829, the earliest rules governing employment were concerned with indentures, since most labour consisted of workers bonded to their employers. The terms of these agreements were not

* In 1953, F.W. Crowley, a Senior Lecturer at the University of Western Australia, published a two-part history of the Master and Servant law in Western Australia, in the *Journal and Proceedings of the Western Australian Historical Society* (Volume IV Parts V and VI). Since then no further study of the law has been undertaken and Crowley's pioneering work has been held to be authoritative. The current paper seeks to enlarge the scope of Crowley's research by correcting some mistakes, introducing new facts and occasionally interpreting events differently.

always the same, there being differences in the period for which servants were bonded, in whether they had to repay their passage money and in the wage rates contracted for.

As no legal system existed in the new colony when it was first established, Governor Sir James Stirling issued a Proclamation on the 28th August 1829, whereby "the country became subject to the laws of the United Kingdom."[1] This was approved and applauded by the Colonial Office[2] but it was apparent that it could not be more than an interim measure and that more specific laws and a structure for enforcing them would soon have to be set in place. This was particularly so in the sphere of labour relations, where there appeared to be some misunderstanding as to the validity of the contracts between masters and servants arriving in the colony.[3] While it was accepted that the laws of England were henceforth to apply, there was doubt whether existing obligations under that law could also be transferred to Western Australia and hence whether indentures were legal.

To overcome this uncertainty Governor Stirling issued a further Proclamation on 17th November 1829 which dealt almost solely with questions surrounding indentures and sought generally to legitimise them.[4] Thereafter, all indentures of service had to be registered at the Colonial Secretary's office immediately upon arrival. Any who wished to hire workers locally, would then know by application at the Secretary's office the names of servants who were bound by previous indentures, and those who sought to employ persons already indentured without consent of their legitimate masters were made liable to a penalty of £100. All complaints of misconduct by servants or of breach of contract by masters in matters pertaining to food, lodging or treatment, were to be made in writing to the Colonial Secretary, who would then hold an inquiry on a specified day. A result of these stipulations was that the Colonial Secretary assumed responsibility for the proper administration of the indentured-labour system and in the process had also to serve as a legal officer, there being no magistracy in the Colony.

The final third of the Proclamation contained a summary of the law of Masters and Servants which employers were instructed to pass on to their employees. The law enjoined the master to perform his part of the contract "by supplying good and sufficient food, lodging and such other articles as may have been agreed upon" and to require from his servants "such labour only as they may have consented to render him and during such hours only as was customary in their respective branches of labour."

The penalties for non-observance of the law were markedly tilted in favour of the masters. If a master broke his contract, the Government, upon this being proved, could discharge the servant from further fulfilment of the conditions of the agreement. But what if the master broke his contract by defaulting on wages? Of many possible misdemeanours this would have been the most serious to the servant as it undermined the main reason for his being in the colony. Yet, there was no provision in the law that the arrears should be paid. In fact, wage default was nowhere mentioned in the Governor's Proclamation.

Servants, on the other hand, were bound by a variety of rules which gave both latitude and immense power to their employers. Idleness, insolence, negligence and disobedience were considered breaches of contract but were undefined in the law and so open to doubtful interpretation. Consequently, claims for better treatment or higher wages could be regarded as a manifestation of "insolence" and the results of flood and drought laid at the door of "negligence." If adjudged proved upon complaint by the masters, the government could authorise masters to stop all further issue of provisions and wages and to turn offenders off their premises. These offences also rendered the servant liable to prosecution and imprisonment until any financial penalties which may have been imposed in addition had been paid off.

A number of further conditions made it virtually impossible for the normal run of indentured servants to effect a quick improvement in their status. They could not hold grants of land until their indentures had been served; no servant, unless regularly discharged could be employed by any other person, and no-one under indenture was permitted to leave the colony during its term.[5]

Enforcement of the law required the beginnings of a judicial administration and Stirling's hand was quickened by the arrival in December 1829 of a number of indentured servants "whose habits were of the loosest description." To control them and to protect their masters and the general public, the Governor moved before year's end to appoint a magistracy and a body of constables. The class composition of the two categories reflected well the social attitudes of the time, the magistrates being drawn from the "most wealthy and prudent of the settlers" and the constables from "the steady and most respectable part of the working-class."[6]

The magistrates (who confusingly were also known as Justices of the Peace in these early years, the designations being used synonymously) soon discovered that the most frequent disputes between masters and servants arose over disagreements about working hours and rations. Stirling's Proclamation of 1829 had touched on both subjects, but the principles laid down were far too general, *i.e.*, "good and sufficient food" and "customary hours of labour," left so much room for interpretation that they were next to useless. Firmly established standards were needed and putting these in place became one of the earliest tasks of the magistracy.

At the end of February 1830, scales of hours and rations were drawn up for the sanction of the Governor. The working hours proposed for mechanics and labourers engaged in husbandry — the latter being the category into which most indentured labourers fell — made allowances for the weather and were set at 8 hours a day in the hot season from the 15th November to the 15th of February and 9 hours a day over the rest of the year. Two further problems which had begun to emerge were dealt with at the same time. Servants who absented themselves without leave or were incapacitated by drunkenness had to compensate for the time lost at the rate of wages then current in the colony; and no servant without the previous consent of his master was permitted to work for any other person, even though such work was done during extra hours.[7]

Scales of daily food rations spelt out the different quantities which masters were obliged to supply to their servants, except in the case of an agreement in writing to the contrary, though this was relatively rare. There was no difference in the value or quantity of food-stuffs apportioned to adult men and women, except that the latter received tea and sugar in lieu of rum. Children were put into a number of age categories with each entitled to a proportion of an adult's ration.[8]

Though prepared to approve the working hours stipulated by the magistrates, Stirling refused to accept the victualling scale in its entirety. With a show of compassion, a trait with which he is not often credited, the Governor declared that he did not "... conceive the specified scales sufficient for the working class without some additional comforts," particularly in the existing state of the colony, where servants had "many privations and difficulties to encounter, which they would not have in the Mother Country."[9]

The victualling scale of which the Governor approved was both more liberal and more elaborate than that proposed by the magistrates and along with the arrangements covering working hours were incorporated in a Proclamation on 26th March 1830.[10] The principles embodied in the Proclamation were of considerable significance in that they set basic standards for working hours and diet which employers of indentured labour had to observe. On the surface they appear to contradict the principles of *laissez faire* teaching, which opposed intervention in the work-place, but to hold such a view would be to deny a positive character to the laissez faire credo and treat it as a synonym for anarchism. Those who supported the theory were not attempting to whittle away all forms of government control in the belief that an administrative nihilism was a desirable ideal. What they aspired to was a minimum framework of law and order within which the play of economic forces could produce the good of all. With time this relatively simple concept grew in sophistication and content. Official endeavours to apply the theory to the economic life of England tended to erode its earlier rigidity and gave to *laissez faire* a practical dynamism it had previously lacked. The philosophy, in other words, matured with age and during the process acquired a more accommodating attitude towards certain facets of the minimum framework it sought to establish. One such embraced its approach to the question of labour legislation. In the last quarter of the 18th Century all forms of interference in this field had been condemned, but by 1802, it had come to be accepted that legislation on behalf of orphan children employed in the factories of Britain, was not contrary to the laissez faire spirit, since this category of labour was too helpless to promote its own advantage. With the passing years the scope of this 'helpless' category was extended, first to cover all employed children — whether orphaned or not, and later to cover women and "young persons" as well. It is apparent that the Colonial Office had decided that immigrant labour, even when adult fell under the classification of "helpless" and that legislation in its interests was a duty which the state could scarcely avoid. This being the ruling approach in the early 19th Century, it would be far from correct to consider Stirling's proclamation of 1830 a transgression of the *laissez faire* code.

However, the Proclamation and its contents were not destined to last for long. A little over two years later, in July 1832, Stirling repealed the Proclamation by public notice.[11] Crowley argues that this was done because the provision of spirits by masters as stipulated by the Governor's victualling scale violated an Act of Council which forbade employers to pay their servants' wages wholly or in part with "spirituous and fermented liquors."[12]

It is difficult to agree with Crowley's explanation of events. Rations were distributed to those whose contracts did not specifically include the supply of food, irrespective of whether they were paid wages or not. Moreover, nowhere in the Proclamation was it suggested that rations could be issued in lieu of wage payments. Crowley appears to have confused the effects of two acts, passed within a month of one another. "An act to regulate the sale of spirituous and fermented liquors by retail" — 2nd William IV, No. 8 — was passed by Council on the 8th of May 1832 and clause V therein forbade the payment of wages in liquor. The second act, 2nd William IV No. 10 was passed by Council on the 9th of June 1832. "To impose certain duties on imported and spirituous liquors." Clauses I and II decreed that duties of 3 sh. and 4 sh. per imperial gallon should be levied on spirits imported from the UK and foreign countries respectively. That it was the latter act which led to the scuttling of the ration scheme is borne out by the proceedings of the Executive Council at its meeting of 29th June 1832. The Minutes report that "the Governor called the attention of the Council to a Proclamation related to the rations to be issued to servants dated 26th March 1830, and stated that in consequence of a late Act of Council imposing a duty on spirits, difficulties had presented themselves as to the Masters providing their servants with spirits; he proposed that the Proclamation alluded to be repealed by public notice." Council unanimously agreed.[13]

It must not be missed that the real reason for repeal was a desire to safeguard the economic interests of the masters. The duty on spirits raised the price of the liquor ration and in effect pushed up the real wage rates masters had to pay. This does not seem to have been taken into consideration when the second act of 1832 went before the Executive Council and was successfully passed. The masters were an important socio-economic segment in the new colony, their presence and support vital to its establishment and future success. Their economic viability as employers had therefore to be preserved and this clearly was Stirling's objective when he sought to rectify the Council's oversight.

The repeal of the Proclamation also had implications that reached well beyond the matter of rations and customs duties. The control over working hours it had established was removed at a stroke and the result was that indentured workers found themselves back where they had been in March 1830, bereft of protection in two of the areas where it mattered most, working hours and rations.

Advent of Locally-based Master and Servant Laws

With the repeal of the Proclamation all colonial regulations on the relationship between master and servant ceased to exist. Thereafter, Justices of the Peace fell back on the English law as proclaimed by Governor Stirling in November 1829. Problems of interpretation arose from time to time, but these were overcome through the Justices using their knowledge of local needs and conditions. Early in 1840 however, a decision in an English court created difficulties in the continued use of the English law of Master and Servant in Western Australia. The Court of the King's Bench in England decided that Justices of the Peace had no authority to hear complaints between domestic servants and their masters. This meant that neither master nor servant could be dealt with summarily and hence cheaply, but had to resort to the expense of an action in a law court or a Court of Requests.[14] To overcome this shortcoming the Legislative Council introduced legislation which extended the jurisdiction of magistrates in cases between masters and servants, *i.e.*, it gave to the magistrates in the Colony powers which were no longer possessed by their counterparts in England. The Act itself was short, but extremely comprehensive in that it empowered magistrates "to hear and determine all cases of complaint by or against Masters and Servants of every description, whether domestic servants, servants in husbandry, or any other sort of servants, or by or against artificers, workmen, and labourers of every description employed to perform any work, whether by the hour, or by the day, or in any other manner in respect of time, or by the piece, or the job, or in any other manner in respect of work."[15]

The new bill made legislative history. When passed by Council on 2nd July 1840, it became the first Master and Servant Act to have originated in the Colony. But Whitehall had serious reservations about the comprehensive nature of the bill and these proved strong enough for Secretary of State Lord John Russell to refuse its passage. As Russell saw it, there were two major objections to the bill. Firstly, it was to apply "to servants of every description whatever may be the nature of their service, and to labourers of every description employed to perform any work, whatever may be the nature of work of the employment." Such a specification would embrace a very high proportion of society *i.e.*, "all mechanics, all artisans, all apprentices, all persons employed in shops or in agriculture, all persons hired to write and perhaps everyone engaged in employment purely intellectual or partly so, as compositors, merchants, clerks and so on through innumerable illustrations". All such persons could be brought under the control of a Justice of the Peace and subjected to fines and imprisonment on a summary conviction for breach or neglect of contract of services. This was thought to be too far-reaching and its implications to take it, quite unwittingly, well beyond the intentions of the framers of the Act.

The second objection raised by the Colonial Office concerned the apparent belief reflected in the Act, that there was in England a single general law covering disputes between masters and servants which could be imported wholesale, as it were, to the Colony. In fact, the English law contained a great many exemptions and defined with great care the various classes of labourers to which they extended, with very different regulations for each. The adoption of a general law as envisaged in the bill, would therefore create "a multitude of difficulties and settle none."

The solution suggested by London was that a comprehensive Act should be avoided and that Western Australian legislators should look to the neighbouring Australian colonies for guidance. The latter had faced similar problems and a suitable law could be copied from their statute books.[16] As an example of what was required, an Act passed in Van Dieman's Land, 4 Vic. No. 12 of 1840, was enclosed with the Secretary of State's despatch.[17]

Taking Whitehall at its word Governor Hutt made the Act from Van Dieman's Land the basis of a new bill. Crowley disagrees, holding that this was not done and that Governor Hutt quite "erroneously" informed Secretary of State Lord Stanley that "the ... Act of 1840 had been strictly followed."[18] Reasons for the Governor's behaviour are not suggested, but it is evident that Crowley is mistaken. An examination of the new bill — 6 Victoria, No. 5 of 1842 — shows that large sections, in fact about 80% of the total, was taken directly from the Van Dieman's Land Act. The penalties and remedies proposed are exactly the same, as indeed is the very language in which they are couched. The Western Australian Legislative Council appears merely to have duplicated the bill transmitted to it by the Colonial Office.

Passed on the 25th of August 1842, "to provide a summary remedy in certain cases of Breach of Contract," the new Act, 6 Victoria, No. 5 of 1842, was the first legitimate Master and Servant law in the Colony, though it must be noted that the disallowed Act of 1840 functioned in a *de facto* capacity from its passage in July 1840 until October 1841, when the Secretary of the State's dissent was received.

The Act of 1842 had a widespread but lacked the global reach which had led to its predecessor's undoing. According to its provisions, all proceedings had to be determined in a summary manner before two or more magistrates. Any hired artificer, manufacturer, journeyman, workman, labourer or other servant, employed in any manner, who absented himself or was guilty of any other misconduct, was liable to imprisonment with hard labour, not exceeding three months and to forfeit all or part of his wages. Similarly fencers, well sinkers, mowers, splitters and other labourers on contract for piece or time work, were liable to three months hard labour for failing to fulfil their contracts.

Where complaints were made by servants, whether hired or on contract, of non-payment of wages, cruelty or other ill-treatment, employers could be summoned before any two or more Justices, who could order the payment of such wages as appeared to be owing. Where other forms of misconduct were concerned, the Justices could award such compensation as seemed fair and reasonable, provided that the compensation awarded did not exceed six months wages of a hired servant or half the payment due to a contract worker.

Finally, any person who knowingly employed a servant already hired or on contract, without leave of their employers could be charged a penalty of up to £50.

The Act of 1842, like the regulations laid down by the Proclamations that preceded it, favoured master above servant. As shown above, the penalties, both penal and financial, for breach of contract by workers were heavy *i.e.*, three months in jail with hard labour and loss of all or part of wages due; whereas employers were never to be punished with imprisonment and were only liable for wages due, or in cases of maltreatment, for compensation that was not in excess of six months wages.

Nonetheless, one important advance on the part of the servants must be noted. Prior to the Act a servant's rights to wages due had not been established and redress could only be secured by resorting to the ordinary processes of the law — a course most could not afford. In 1842, that injustice was corrected and funds for wages in default or as compensation for ill-treatment could be raised through sale of the goods and effects of the employer.[19]

A notable characteristic of the Act was that it was mainly limited to a concern with the contract to work. In keeping with *laissez faire* tenets as they had developed through the first decade of the 19th Century in the field of labour relations, it showed a willingness to intercede on behalf of the weak, but at a minimum level. Given the inequalities of the existing socio-economic framework this limited intercession was far from sufficient to preserve the balance and permitted the advantage to remain in the hands of those in power.

The essentials of the bill of 1842 remained more or less intact for a full 50 years. As the century progressed the practice of indenturing labour gradually died down and it became more common to hire workers locally on short-term agreements rather than bring them in from abroad. This growth of a locally recruited labour force was hastened during and after the convict period 1850-1868 — as expires, ticket-of-leave and conditional pardon men sought employment in the colony, and as natural increase and free immigration proceeded steadily. The change in the nature of the workforce, did not at first seriously interfere with the working of the Master and Servant law, since employment was still based on individual agreements between employer and employee. But the continued expansion of the economy brought complex problems in its wake and made necessary a number of adjustments and additions to the law which ultimately altered its very nature.

A new element which increasingly entered the labour market was the aboriginal worker. Engaged to undertake a variety of unskilled operations, their presence in the workforce grew from about the middle of the century. At first, labour was simply exchanged for food and drink, but before long more formal arrangements emerged and the payment of money wages grew widespread. This in turn brought bargaining and dispute in its train and it became common practice for employers to seek written agreements which could be proven in a court of law. These agreements, resembling the indentures binding white labourers, were attested by the individual's "mark" and witnessed by a third party.

The legal position of aboriginal workers under these contracts was thought to be no different from that of white servants and hence governed by the current Master and Servant law of 1842. The same penalties applied, it being assumed that there was no difference other than colour between the two parties. That a wide cultural gulf divided them was totally ignored, and to the bias that already existed against all workers more shortcomings were added when the law was applied to the indigenous population. An aboriginal if ill-treated or unhappy in his work would almost never avail himself of legal avenues of protest; his usual reaction would be to desert and take to the bush. According to the law he could then be bought back and punished as an absconder, with up to three months, imprisonment with hard labour, and if applicable, with the forfeiture of all or part of his wages due. In other words "the plaintiff" was transformed into "the accused" by the vagaries of the legal system. Whereas under the law the white worker had opportunities for a modicum of redress, and beyond that the right of appeal to a higher court, the aboriginal though covered by the same enactment lacked the understanding to take advantage of the protective sections of the Act. A noticeable ambiguity therefore crept into the Master and Servant law in its application to servants. There were now three players on the stage — masters, white servants and black servants — and to the differences in treatment between master and servant were added those between black and white.

Master and Servant in a Growing Economy

In 1850 Western Australia became a penal settlement for the first time in its history. Two recurrent problems since foundation in 1829 had been the shortage of labour and the dearth of capital and by the late 1840's opinion in the colony had come to accept that the introduction of convicts and the imperial expenditure on the convict establishment that would follow, would solve both problems by injecting men and money into the economy. London was sympathetic, seeing it as an opportunity for lessening the pressure on English jails and by the middle of 1850 Western Australia had become a convict destination. Between that date and 1868, when the practice was discontinued, a total of 9,669 convicts had been landed in Perth.[20]

After their arrival in the colony the convicts were at first entirely under the control of Government and were normally employed on public works. With good behaviour they qualified for tickets-of-leave, after which their services were available to the colonists. Following a further spell of probation as ticket-of-leave holders the convicts could win a conditional pardon and with this they entered the labour market on the same terms as an ordinary citizen. Yet another period of trial followed, after which the convicts gained their complete freedom as time-expired prisoners and then, theoretically at least, were the equal of anyone in the country.[21] In the first of these penal states the convicts were governed by the rules and regulations of the prison authorities, but once out of jail on tickets-of-leave, conditional pardons or as expirees, they became part of the workforce and hence were covered by the Masters and Servants Law.

To neutralise the numerical presence of the convicts and simultaneously to bolster the size of the Western Australian population, a policy of assisting immigration to the colony was launched in 1850. Unassisted immigration, though on a much smaller scale, also took place and by the end of the convict period in 1868 these two categories along with natural increase had added some 10,000 additional citizens. There was some leakage through re-emigration and deaths, but the colony's population, which at the start of the penal era had totalled 5,886 had risen to 24,292 when it ended.[22]

The expansion of the population base was accompanied by a growth in the economy. A reduction in the price of crown lands from £1 to 10 sh. per acre led to a marked extension in the acreage under crop, which tripled in the 15 years 1856-1870, while over the same period large stretches of good pastoral land were opened up in the north-west.[23] Both developments led to a dispersion of the labour force away from Perth and on the pastoral front in particular it was soon believed that a stiffening of the Masters and Servants law was necessary. In the words of the Attorney-General "large and valuable flocks and herds were being left in charge of a class of servants not notorious for over-carefulness" and it was thought justifiable that legislation more severe than the Masters and Servants laws then in force should be enacted.[24] Clearly, the reference here is to the large numbers of ticket-of-leave and conditional-pardon men who by 1868 had taken employment as shepherds and cow-herds and moved out into the countryside.

In August 1869, Ordinance No. 8 "... further to provide summary remedy between Masters and Servants" was unanimously approved by the Legislative Council and then similarly sanctioned by the Colonial Office. The Ordinance augmented the existing Act of 1842 by providing compensation to both masters and servants for losses which might arise out of their relationship. It again drew attention to the "heavy losses through the wilful and careless conduct of their servants" which masters allegedly suffered and went on to specify that servants who wilfully or negligently damaged livestock and property committed to their charge, could be compelled to pay reasonable damages. In default, offenders could be sent to goal for up to six months, with or without hard labour, could be deprived of all or part of their wages and if the employer so wished, could be discharged from employment.[25]

The Ordinance also had something in it for servants, aiding them with provisions which compensated for the payment of wages in cheques, drafts, orders or notes which were subsequently dishonoured; the servant being empowered to recover the principal due, together with damages, interest and costs.[26] On balance however, the new legislation retained a bias in favour of the masters. The latter could recover damages, seize wages and send a defaulting servant to prison with hard labour, whereas servants could never win goal sentences against their employers, having to accept monetary compensation alone.

A further example of bias is to be found in a clause of Ordinance 8 which made servants liable for damages if any livestock they were in charge of were injured or destroyed by poisonous herbage.[27] As one writer put it, servants were to be punished "for not knowing what their masters in most cases did not know either — which herbage was poisonous and which not."[28]

One of the more interesting developments in the history of Masters and Servants legislation in Western Australia occurred in 1873 with an incident which appears to have escaped the notice of Labour Historians. By early 1873 serious doubts had arisen in the colony as to whether there was any law in force by which persons under-age could bind themselves as apprentices to master-workman — a practice which was then widespread. Notice was accordingly given in Council that a question seeking to clarify the issue would be put to the Attorney-General. The latter believed that in fact there was no such law, but was advised that if he publicly tendered such an answer in Council, there would be a general strike of the apprentices who would see themselves bereft of legality and hence security. In the circumstances, discussion of the issue in the House had to be avoided and legitimisation of apprenticeships effected without the matter being specifically debated in the Council. This was achieved through the ingenious expedient of adopting wholesale — in Ordinance 12 of 1874, which was hurried through the Council — all the laws then in force in England relating to Masters and Apprentices. A step which automatically legalised the latter.[29]

Had the threatened apprentices strike occurred, it would have made history as the first example of direct industrial action in the colony's history. Strikes require planning, particularly if the numbers involved are large and there is reason to believe that they were, given the alarm of the Attorney-General. Yet, there is no evidence of even the rudiments of an organisation capable of planning a strike and no reference to any aspect of the incident in the newspapers of the time. In the 1870's strikes were of course, known in the U.K. and Ireland, where most immigrants originated and the notion could certainly have been carried by them to Western Australia.

The Pearling Industry and Experiments with Aboriginal Labour

The development of the pearl-fishing industry in the early 1860's led in its first stages to a considerable employment of aboriginal labour under conditions which existing Master and Servant legislation did not adequately cover.

Initially, the industry was restricted to the collection of oysters by hand, from reefs and shallows during low tide. When these had been fished out, operations moved into deeper waters and diving off boats, though without the aid of special apparatus, became the usual practice. Up to this time the divers were almost entirely aboriginals and their employers were often land holders upon whose property the aboriginals lived. The terms of employment comprised the exchange of labour for a nominal wage, the latter made up usually of food. Both parties regarded the arrangement with favour. The aboriginal, since he was assured of a regular food supply and the employer, since labour was cheap and ready to hand.

To meet the exigencies created by aboriginal employment a number of ordinances were passed in rapid succession between 1871 and 1883, creating a body of labour laws supplementary to existing Master and Servant legislation, but relating largely to aboriginal workers in the Pearling industry. The first of these ordinances, No. 14 of 1871 ruled that contracts of service had to be in writing and witnessed by certain specified persons e.g. Police Constables and Justices of the Peace; failure by the employer to enter into such an agreement being punishable by a fine of up to £10. The agreement, duly dated and signed by both employer and aboriginal had to clearly describe the nature and duration of the engagement, the time at which work was to begin and the amount of wages to be paid. A further stipulation was that employers should return aboriginal workers to the places where they had been first engaged. This was an important requirement as Pearling Masters were known to hire aboriginals, take them pearling and then, rather than feed and maintain them on the way back, put them ashore 50 miles or more away from their homes. In disputes arising out of the enforcement of these regulations, Justices of the Peace were empowered to impose on either party a penalty of up to £30 and to punish those who defaulted in their payments with imprisonment not exceeding three months, with or without hard labour. The ordinance also prohibited the employment on board of aboriginal females. They were the best divers but their presence led to frequent quarrels "with the white people, in consequence of the females being taken away not for pearling, but for other purposes". To stamp out this practice, masters found with women on board ship were made liable for a penalty of up to £50 for every such offence, a quite heavy impost for those times.

The Ordinances subsequently passed, *i.e.,* in 1873, 1875 and 1883, were in effect refinements of the 1871 Act, filling out many of its provisions. Ordinance 11 of 1873 improved the form of the agreement and introduced clauses which sought to make certain that aboriginal workers were free and voluntary agents, that they understood the agreement and were physically fit for the work they were employed to do. All proposed agreements were limited to 12 months at a maximum and certain persons, *i.e.,* JPs, Customs Officers and Police Officers, were empowered to board and stop pearling schooners to check whether agreements were being properly observed. They were also required to investigate whether the vessels were adequately provisioned, and allowed to restrain them until satisfied that they were; the penalty for disobeying any order in this regard, ranged between £20 and £50.

Two years later Ordinance 13 of 1875 brought more controls over living conditions on pearling vessels. The Governor was given power to make regulations regarding the accommodation provided on board and the number of persons each vessel was permitted to carry. The times at which diving could be carried on was also brought under the Act, and was really a thinly veiled attempt at preventing work on Sundays so as "to ensure a more proper observance of the sanctity of the Sabbath" by putting "an end to the existing practice of employing natives ... to dive for shells on Sunday, regardless of their physical and moral welfare." Persons violating any of the new regulations were deemed guilty of an offence and subject to a fine of up to £20.

Ordinance 13 ran into a surprising degree of resistance in the Legislative Council, objections being levelled at the granting of "unlimited and somewhat vaguely defined powers to the Executive." As the reference here was to the Governor, the Officials in Council closed ranks, countered all opposition and the Act passed into the law of the land.

The aboriginal presence in the pearling industry began to decline in the 1870's. As diving continued to move out into ever-deepening waters, Pearling Masters came to prefer the services of Philipinos and Timorese on the grounds that they had the ability to stay under water for longer periods; and then with a change in technology to employ diving-suit clad Japanese. The law accommodated these changes and Ordinance 10 of 1883 acknowledged the new methods of pearling by amending the Act of 1875 to include the words "otherwise collecting" after the words "diving for". As the demand for aboriginal labour in the pearling industry fell away, their presence in the workforce contracted rapidly and the introduction of special legislation covering the conditions of aboriginal employment in it came to an end.

Legal Adjustments in a Maturing Economy

After transportation ended in 1868 the convict strain in the Western Australian population diminished rapidly. The census of 1870 showed a total of only 3,958 persons for all categories of transportees in the colony and their number continued to fall rapidly as expirees moved out seeking the anonymity of living in the eastern colonies.[30] Nonetheless, population kept on rising, going from 24,785 in 1870 (census) to 29,708 in 1881 (census), driven now by natural growth and immigration and not by transportation and indenture. The alteration in the social make-up of the population appears to have brought about a slight shift in the attitude towards worker and peasant. One finds fewer criticisms of their quality than previously and the adoption of a softer approach in dealing with them becomes apparent. An escalating demand for labour after the late 1870's also contributed to the change. It led to a re-appraisal of the immigration system and to an attempt to make working conditions in Western Australia more attractive.[31]

One such step was a small modification in the Master and Servants Law in favour of the servants. In 1882, Ordinance 22 repealed the provision introduced by Ordinance 5 of 1842 and still in force, which made obligatory, the imprisonment of servants who breached a contract. Thereafter, Judges were given discretion to either imprison or else impose a penalty not exceeding £10.[32] The alteration, though slight, was of considerable significance since it was the first change in the law with the express intention of alleviating the legal disabilities of employees. On the other hand, too much should not be read into the concession. A telling incident in Parliament during the preparation of the Ordinance showed that in a fundamental sense the attitude to servants though better had only improved marginally. At the third reading of the bill the Attorney-General pointed out that the proposed change in the wording of the clause relating to breaches of contract "... would render masters as well as their servants liable to a fine on imprisonment. The object of the bill of course, was to punish servants." The clause was accordingly reworded so as to make certain that its original intent was achieved.[33]

After 1882 the tensions that were developing in Western Australian society continued to grow. The rate of immigration increased, yet fell far short of the demand for labour created by an improving economy. As it became apparent that organisation was an advantage when labour was short, the colony's first trade union appeared in 1884 and at the same time rudimentary political parties began to form and to press, amongst other things, for the introduction of responsible government.

These changing social forces brought a further push against the Masters and Servants law in their train. In 1884, the Government, keen to build up labour supplies through enhanced immigration, moved to amend the laws yet again, bringing them in line with those in force in England and certain of the other Australian colonies. Under these laws breaches of contract by servants were no longer looked upon as a crime, but simply as a breach of an agreement entered into between contracting parties. Those who broke contracts could be called upon to make good the damages that may have accrued as a result of their actions. A law was, therefore, proposed in 1884, to apply equally to the employer and the employed. Hence, "it sought to put workmen and workwomen on an equality with their wealthier neighbours and to provide one and the same law for the rich and the poor."[34] There was considerable point in this comment, for as the law then stood, servants who broke their contracts could be sent to gaol, but not masters who did likewise. In other words while the agreement between master and servant was a civil question and was always treated as such when a master was involved, a breach by a servant was converted into a criminal offence and carried harsher penalties. The bill sought to rectify this shortcoming, by ensuring that labour had equal rights with the employer.

If the Government felt that the liberalisation of master-servant relations would serve the colony's interests by attracting potential immigrants, the non-Governmental members of the Legislative Council thought otherwise. They unanimously opposed the bill on the grounds that its provisions were not applicable since "the circumstances in Western Australia and the state of its labour market were entirely different from the circumstances and condition of the labour market in England or in the other colonies." This stance was supported by two major arguments. The first was that if servants were given the privilege of a civil action in respect of breaches of contract, Judges would have to impose fines or seize their goods and chattels so as to compensate their masters. But most servants had little money and no chattels beyond a "tin pannikin and a rug," and "what satisfaction would this afford to their employers."[35]

The second criticism was that the bill would apply to coloured labour as well as white. In the north-west a large number of servants were aboriginals, while a high proportion of the remainder were either Malays or Chinese. How, it was asked, would an aboriginal who breached an agreement be dealt with? Under the existing law he would be arrested and imprisoned, but under the proposed act he would have to be summoned to appear in court. This would be difficult to effect since aboriginal workers "were here today and there tomorrow." Where the Malays and Chinese were concerned, they were brought out by their employers at their own expense and for the first 12 months or so were largely in their debt. If they broke their contracts and absconded it would be impossible to press a civil action against them, whereas they could be held to their contracts by the threat of imprisonment through criminal proceedings. Given the hostility these opinions show, it is not surprising that the bill was defeated by 16 votes to 4 — only the Government members voting in its favour.[36]

The arguments put up in favour of maintaining the status quo reflect the desire to retain control over a deficient labour supply and the belief that it could best be done by instilling the fear of imprisonment into the worker. This view was strongly supported in the press, which lamented the spirit of "radical sentimentalism" that prompted the Government to further "measures such as either the country does not require or are positively opposed to its interests, merely because they happen in the mother country to be law."[37]

New Attitudes and New Approaches

The inflexible attitudes expressed in the opposition to the proposed legislation of 1884 changed remarkably in the short space of two years. By 1886 the Western Australian-born had become the largest segment of the population and net immigration had increased markedly. As free labour became the norm the quality of the labour pool continued to improve and with it the belief that the threat of incarceration had a positive influence on the efficacy of contractual employment began to recede. The upshot was that a Master and Servant law which took a more liberal attitude to breaches of contract was allowed to pass unchallenged through the legislature. Ordinance 20 of 1886 dealt with the provision in the preceding Masters and Servants law of 1882 which made it discretionary on the part of the Justice trying the case to impose a penalty of imprisonment or to fine an offending servant. The new bill took away the discretionary power of imprisonment in the first instance and empowered the magistrate only to inflict a fine. If the fine was not paid then alone could the offender be imprisoned with or without hard labour, the size of the unpaid fine deciding the period of imprisonment, *i.e.*, one month for fines of £10 or less, two months for £10 to £25 and three months for sums above £25.[38]

Though Ordinance 20 was in advance of previous Masters and Servants laws, it ignored their failure to impose the penalty of imprisonment upon masters, the other party to the employment contract, for any breach on their part. This was class legislation at its worst and even the Government soon came to accept that the laws were iniquitous and that they quite rightly, "occasioned a great deal of raucous feeling in the minds of the artisan and working classes of the community." This observation made in the legislature by an unofficial member, is of considerable significance, being an early indication of dissatisfaction and protest welling up from below.[39] However, as demonstrated in Ordinance 20, the solution to the problem was not thought to lie in so changing the law as to imprison all defaulters with an even hand, be they masters or servants. In the interests of getting the bill accepted, the Government softened its earlier stance, compromised with the local establishment and merely made it more difficult to imprison servants, while leaving untouched the privileged position of the master.

In the meantime, settlement in the north-west of Western Australia progressed rapidly, and with it the expansion of aboriginal employment on the farms and stations. The growing workforce, both black and white, fell initially under the Master and Servant laws, but as the coloured segment grew, the government concluded that as in the pearling industry, aboriginal workers in other fields had, for a variety of reasons, mainly cultural, to be rather differently treated. In 1886 therefore, Ordinance 25 of that year, "The Aborigines Protection Act" was passed and thereafter functioned alongside the Master and Servant laws "to provide for the better protection and management of the Aboriginal Natives of Western Australia and to amend the law relating to certain contracts with such Aboriginal Natives."[40] As the title indicates the bill went well beyond the concerns of the Master and Servant Law. In its broader objectives it frequently impinged on the relationship between employer and employee and so must be examined in some detail.

The new Act was divided into five parts, all of which were concerned with aboriginal labour and touched existing Master and Servant legislation. The first portion set up an Aborigines Protection Board to supervise all matters affecting aboriginals. To accomplish this, a number of Native Protectors were appointed by the Board to scrutinise contracts entered into by aborigines, to look after their welfare and to enforce the law on their behalf. The second portion of the bill related to the form of the contracts. It held that no contract was valid unless it was in writing and the signatory was over 14 years old. The contract had to be signed or marked by the employer and by the aboriginal worker, had to specify the nature of the service and the period of time over which it extended, and had to stipulate that employers would supply sufficient rations, clothing, blankets and medicines to their aboriginal employees.

All valid contracts had to be witnessed by a Justice of the Peace, a Protector of Aboriginals or some "fit and proper person" appointed by the Resident Magistrate of the relevant district. The last provision had inherent shortcomings, since the individual selected could be a friend of the employer and choose to close his eyes to deficiencies in the agreement, *e.g.*, concerning the supply of food, medicines, etc. Nevertheless, it was the best arrangement available under existing circumstances. North-Western Australia was so vast and habitations so widely scattered that Justices of the Peace and Protectors may not have been readily accessible to would-be employers. The bill did not prevent settlers in the outlying districts from making any contract they wished with an aboriginal, but in case of default they could not enforce the terms of the contract through a law-court, unless it had been correctly witnessed and signed, by one of the persons specified in the Act.

Experience had shown that while aboriginals were prepared to work for wages at a variety of jobs, they appeared to find continuous labour irksome and had a tendency to go "walkabout", *i.e.*, return to the bush for short periods. According to the Master and Servant Law, these absences constituted violations of contract, for which penalties could be exacted, with defaulters being sought out, forcibly brought back by the police and sentenced to a period of imprisonment. Since money and time would be spent on persons who were after all, willing to re-enter the workforce after a short break, the new Act decided to overcome the problem by avoiding it. Provision for the trait of occasional absence was built into the law by requiring employers to grant aboriginals a leave of absence of 14-30 days for every working period of 3 months to 6 months respectively. This arrangement was accepted without adverse comment when the bill went before the Legislature, employers seeing that much else could not be done.

Where employers failed to observe the terms of a contract, or ill-treated their aboriginal workers, contracts could be immediately cancelled by a Justice of the Peace. To verify whether the terms of a contract were being observed, Protectors of Aborigines were authorised to enter premises where aborigines were engaged or resided. There was considerable opposition to this clause when it was first put in the Legislature and the government was obliged to give an assurance that the private homes of settlers would be exempted from inspection.

The minimum age at which contracts could legally be signed with aboriginals was set at 14 years, though only after considerable debate. It was initially suggested by the Government that 16 years was a reasonable minimum, but this was strenuously opposed in the House. One speaker after another argued that the minimum age should be reduced to 10(!) on the grounds that aboriginals "were ... more tractable and more easily trained in habits of industry, and a native at 10 years old knew as much as a white at sixteen."[41]

The Government argued strongly against the validity of this reasoning, pointing out that the contracting age for a white was 21 years and that the reduction to 16 for aboriginals was already a substantial concession. If a further reduction were allowed, public opinion, not only in the colony but outside it, would look askance at "... a law which permitted a native child 10 years old to be sent to prison for breach of contract."[42] Nonetheless, an attempt to reduce the age limit to 10 years was persisted with and only defeated by 3 votes in a Legislature of 23. The best compromise the Government could get was a contractible age of 14 years, *i.e.*, a full seven years below that deemed appropriate for a young settler![43]

The third part of the new Act covered the employment of aboriginal prisoners. It was decided that aboriginals under sentence could be employed in the service of the government outside the limits of their place of detention. The arrangement was already in occasional use by the Police and Survey departments which used aboriginal prisoners as guides in the northern districts. There was considerable opposition in the Legislature to the practice being more widely employed in the colony, it being argued that the rigours of punishment were being by-passed. However, its obvious advantage as a source of cheap labour ultimately overcame all objections and led to its acceptance.[44]

Part IV of the Act empowered magistrates to put out aboriginal children of "a suitable age" as apprentices to acceptable employments, provided that reasonable provision was made for maintenance, clothing and humane treatment. A scale of punishments was specified for parties found guilty of abuses, *i.e.*, if the mistress, by a fine not exceeding £10; if the master, by a fine not exceeding £10 or imprisonment up to one month; if the apprentice, by imprisonment not exceeding one month. In addition, Justices had authority to cancel indentures and thereby annul apprenticeships. Despite the penal clauses attaching to the employer a bias is still apparent. Defaulting apprentices either lost their positions or went to prison, whereas a master had the option of buying off imprisonment through payment of a fine. Admittedly, giving the same alternative to an aboriginal apprentice was of little practical value, since he seldom had any money, yet, fair treatment required that he be given the choice.

The final section of the Act dealt with a miscellaneous collection of provisions ranging from who was deemed to be an aboriginal, to the right of a Justice of the Peace to order out of town any aboriginal who was not "decently clothed from neck to knee." Of these provisions the most contentious was a clause which modified the Master and Servant Laws. Thereafter, in cases of breach of contract, no aboriginal was liable to a fine exceeding £10 or to any term of imprisonment exceeding one month, with or without hard labour. The main reason given for the change was that it was required on "humane grounds" as "natives could not stand imprisonment and confinement like a white man could, ... a native who was locked up for a month probably suffered as much as a white person who was locked up for three months." When this view was first put in the Legislature it was received with hostility. It was argued that since most aboriginal offenders would be on the stations up north, it would take a number of weeks to bring them in to jail. Most of a prisoner's sentence would have expired before the lock-up was reached and he would either have a greatly shortened sentence to serve or no sentence at all. A further objection to the change was that it discriminated between black and white, as non-aboriginals were liable to three months imprisonment for breach of contract, under the Master and Servant Law.

Both arguments were strenuously and successfully opposed by the Government. The first was met by attention being drawn to the conditions under which aboriginal prisoners were brought to Perth.

The Commissioner of Crown Lands (Hon. J. Forrest). "What generally happened in these cases? The native, when caught, or sentenced, had a chain put around his neck, and was marched down by easy stages, and tied to a tree at night. He thought that after a month of that treatment a native was more badly treated than the white man who had been in jail for that time.

Captain Fawcett. Quite as much punishment as being in prison."

These comments sufficed to silence those in opposition and the clause was put to the House and passed.[45]

The second objection and the Government's reaction to it showed a surprising ignorance of the current state of the law, by all concerned. Those who charged discrimination against whites overlooked the fact that barely a fortnight earlier Ordinance 20 of 1886, had eased the penalties attached to breach of contract in the Master and Servant law. Henceforth, offenders were to be fined in the first instance, and imprisoned only for default of the fine, the amount of which decided the length of the period of imprisonment, *i.e.*, one month for fines of £10, two months for £10 to £25, and three months for fines above £25. Hence only a proportion of those who broke contracts were likely to incur more than a month's imprisonment and even this could be avoided through payment of a fine. The argument put by the Government, that there was no discrimination between aboriginals and whites was equally wrong. As shown above, whites, unlike aboriginals, could be given sentences of more than a month in duration, while aboriginal offenders were now given shorter sentences or maximum fines of £10. As there were few if any who could raise the £10, it followed that aboriginal offenders invariably went to prison. This it will be noted, tied in neatly with Part III of the Aboriginal Protection Act which allowed Government to employ aboriginal prisoners in a number of capacities. Prison sentences ensured the perpetuation of a pool from which labour could be drawn and several members of the Government appealed to the House not to interfere with this clause as it would otherwise be impossible to find recruits for expeditions and surveys and as police assistants in the outback.[46]

The Aboriginal Protection Act then, was a multi-faceted piece of legislation. It set up an administrative apparatus to superintend aboriginal affairs throughout the colony, stiffened the rules governing contracts, introduced regulations controlling apprenticeships, made arrangements for the employment in Government service of aboriginal prisoners and modified the operation of the Master and Servant law with regard to the indigenous population. Nevertheless, it cannot be said that the Act greatly progressed the cause of the aboriginal worker. There were a number of areas where it brought about a definite lowering of their socio-legal standing. For instance, the rules governing contracts were not made compulsory, hence many employers dispensed with contracts altogether and aboriginal workers had no redress when irregularities arose. The Act also legalised aboriginal child labour by making 14 the age at which contracts could be signed with them; a consequence was that a child of 14 could be imprisoned for default. Moreover, as shown earlier, the Act enabled a supply of cheap labour through the jails for certain types of work and the clauses covering apprenticeship came dangerously close to doing the same thing, particularly in the provision of young females as domestic servants, a practice common in the north-west.

The contradictions between the Aboriginal Protection Act and the Master and Servant law relative to contracts, which gave aboriginals lighter sentences than some categories of settlers for the same offence, persisted until 1892. In that year the anomalies were officially recognised and the Aboriginal Protection Act amended by Ordinance 25. The amendment concerned itself solely with the clause dealing with breaches of contract, leaving all other portions of the Act untouched. It was noted that in the existing Masters and Servants Act, aboriginals and settlers were treated alike and that before persons could be imprisoned for breach of contract, they had in the first instance to be fined and imprisoned only if they could not pay. As it was thought unlikely that aboriginals would have the funds with which to pay a fine, it was decided in the 1892 amendment that they should be denied the option and made liable to imprisonment for up to three months, with or without hard labour.[47] With this, aboriginal labour lost an advantage it had briefly secured with the Aboriginal Protection Act and assumed an inferior status to white labour. Considering past events one wonders whether this was not continued so as to ensure labour supplies for surveyors, explorers and the police.

There were some who felt that the penalty imposed by the ordinance was still far too lenient and called for heavier punishment. Aboriginals, it was argued, frequently absconded without notice and left the property of their employers to take care of itself. Whites did not do this and that was good reason why "more severe punishments should be provided in the case of natives." Attempts to force an amendment through on discriminatory lines failed narrowly, but that it should have been tried at all, reflects the prejudices of the time.[48]

There was one area however in which the bill bettered the position of the aboriginal worker. It penalised employers who committed a breach of contract through the imposition of a fine. For any breach such as not supplying sufficient rations or clothing or medicine, an employer was made liable to a penalty of £20. Physical ill-treatment was not brought under the new law and continued to be dealt with under the Aboriginal Protection Act of 1886, or in the alternative, employers could be proceeded against under the Criminal law.

The Last Years of the Master and Servant Law

The pace of change — social, economic and political — quickened dramatically after the middle 80's. The discovery of gold in the Kimberleys (1886), Yilgarn and the Pilbara (1888), the Murchison (1891), Coolgardie (1892) and Kalgoorlie (1893), brought thousands of gold-seekers into Western Australia. The population of the Colony which in 1885 stood at 35,959 rose rapidly, reaching 58,569 in 1892 and 100,514 in 1895. The new migrants came largely from the eastern Australian colonies and amongst other things brought with them a more sophisticated approach to politics and industrial relations than then existed in the West. Largely through their efforts the trade union movement developed rapidly and by 1890 unions had appeared in the docks, the railways, the building trades, the gold mines and the printing industry, while in 1892 the Perth Trades and Labour Council, to co-ordinate trade union action, had been set up. On the political front an Eight Hours Association was established in 1889 and in 1893 the extension of the franchise to all males without the requirement of a property qualification, gave a growing influence to these new entrants on the politico-economic stage.

In the face of these developments it was inevitable that the inequities of the Masters and Servants law should be further chipped away. The rapidly expanding working class had obvious reasons for wanting that result and were fast acquiring the instruments with which to achieve it. Likewise, the employers soon had a similar end in view. The early 90's were tumultuous years in the eastern Australian colonies, with industrial troubles inspired and led by the trade unions. Many of the latter's members subsequently migrated to Western Australia and were now on the goldfields. In the circumstances it appeared sensible that obvious injustices in the law should be repealed from above before demands for their removal came from below. Moreover, on the philosophical front, the prejudice against intervention had begun to disappear. The arguments of the English Idealists, that freedom was not a mere lack of regulation but required the full expression of one's personality, with interference being justified if it helped to promote that result, had begun to erode the teachings of *laissez faire*. Accordingly, the agreements between Masters and Servants were expected to take the interests of both parties into consideration.

In March 1892, Ordinance 28 was passed by the Legislature with the express intention of placing master and servant on a footing of absolute equality in relation to breach of contract.[49] "All through the bill the two are to be found running in association with one another. In the same way as we deal with the servant we deal with the master also, for a breach of contract."[50] This was largely the same Act introduced in 1884 and rejected by the House but now reintroduced with some slight changes. Instead of imposing a fine, with imprisonment to follow in the case of default, the bill provided a number of options which Judges could choose from, *e.g.*, they could order abatement of the whole or a part of the wages due to a servant, or direct fulfilment of the contracts, with an order that the party complained against should find security for the carrying out of the contract, or they could annul the contract, discharge the parties and apportion the amount of wages due, and so on. As a last resort judges were empowered to order imprisonment where the courts' orders had not been obeyed. The main thrust of the bill was that Master and Servant were to be equally treated and that Justices could put both under recognisances to perform their contracts; if they still defaulted, the punishment of imprisonment was to come into operation. Those aggrieved by any conviction under the Act were permitted to appeal to the Supreme Court of Western Australia or one of its Judges, both parties being empowered to vary convictions.

After some discussion it was decided that the Act should not apply to women and children or to aboriginals. The former since they were generally employed on menial tasks under the direction of the mistress of a household, and it was thought that imprisonment for breach of contract would be too severe a punishment for usually petty misdemeanours; the latter, since they were now dealt with in a separate act, *i.e.*, Ordinance 25 of 1892.

The exclusion of aboriginals from the Master and Servant bill marked the end of attempts to include settlers and indigenous inhabitants within the scope of a single piece of legislation covering contractual obligations. The difficulties inherent in such an effort had become so apparent that further experiments ceased and the exercise was totally abandoned. Indeed, the rapidly changing scene in Western Australia, brought on by the continuing gold discoveries and consequent inflow of immigrants led to the whole concept of the Master and Servant law being re-assessed. Consequently, Ordinance

28 of 1892 repealed all previous Masters and Servants laws and was the last Act to be passed under that title in Western Australia. Legislation with a bearing on the conditions and status of labour was admittedly enacted after that date, but the new laws did not cover breaches of contract. They were concerned with a variety of other problems likely to arise in the work-place — *e.g.*, employers liability, wage security, hours of work and payments in kind. The enactment of these laws gradually gave new meaning to the individual contract, which lay at the heart of the Master and Servant laws and prepared the ground for the acceptance of the Industrial Conciliation and Arbitration system which came in the 20th century to characterise industrial relations in Australia, of which the West became a part with Federation in 1901.

REFERENCES

1. C.O., 18.3 10th September 1829 — Stirling to Murray.
2. C.O., 397.2 30th May 1830 Murray to Stirling.
3. W.A.A./C.S.F., 16/217-224.
4. C.S.O., 1.49, pp. 217-24 — Proclamation of 17th November, 1829.
5. *Ibid.*
6. C.O., 18.7 20th January 1830 — Stirling to Secretary of State.
7. C.S.R., Vol. 5, p. 92.
8. *Ibid.*
9. C.S.O., 2.49 Letter of 24th March, 1830 from Colonial Secretary to Mr H. Mackie.
10. The victualling scales proposed by the Magistrates (C.S.R. 5.92) — were as follows:

    Rations for a Man servant:

    Beef - one pound per day.
    Pork - three quarters of a pound per day.
    Biscuits / Flour or / Bread } - one pound per day.
    Spirits - half a gill per day.
    Rice may be substituted (at the option of the master) for biscuit or bread or flour. } In the proportion of 1-1/2 lbs of rice for 1 lb of flour, bread or biscuit — to the amount of one half the daily ration.

    Rations for a Woman servant:

    The same as for a man servant, except in the article of rum, of which female servants are to have none, but in lieu thereof, are to have, of

Sugar - half a pound a week.
Tea - two ounces a week.

Rations for Children:

Above 14 years of age	The same as an adult.
From 10 years to 14	Half the full ration of an adult.
From 7 years to 10	One third of full ration.
Below 7 years	One fourth of full ration.

The victualling scales approved by the Governor in the Proclamation of 26 March 1930 were as follows:

Daily Rations for Adults both men and women above 16 years of age:

Wheaten Bread	One pound.
Sugar	One and a half ounces.
Fresh meat	One pound.
Vegetables	Half pound.
Tea	Quarter of an ounce.
Spirits	Half a gill.

When fresh meat and vegetables were not issued there shall be allowed in lieu:

Salt beef	3/4 lb]
Flour	3/4 lb]
Salt Pork	3/4 lb]
Pease (sic)	1/2 lb]
Vinegar	1/2 pint — weekly.
Fish, salt or fresh	2 lbs weekly.

On the days on which flour may be issued, suet and raisins or currants may be substituted for a portion of flour at the following rate. One pound of raisins being considered equal to one pound of flour.

Half pound currants and Half pound suet	equal to one pound of flour.

In case it should be found necessary to alter any of the above species of provisions and to issue others as their substitutes, it is to be observed that:

1-1/4 lb of soft bread or 1 lb of flour	is to be considered equal to one pound biscuit.
1 lb of rice 1 pint of maize	is to be considered equal to one pint of peas.

Rations for Children

From 10 to 16 years -	Half the full ration of an adult except spirits.
From 7 to 10 years -	1/3 the above.
Under 7 years -	1/4 the above.

11. C.O., 20.1 — Minutes of the meeting of the Executive Council of 29th June, 1832.
12. F.K. Crowley — "Master and Servant in Western Australia 1829-1851" — Journal and Proceedings of the Western Australian Historical Society Inc., Volume four, Part V, p. 100.
13. C.O., 20.1 — Minutes of the meeting of the Executive Council of 29th June, 1832.
14. C.O., 18.25 — Hutt to Russell. 19th August 1840.
15. 4 Victoria, No. 2.
16. C.O., 397.5 30th June 1841 — Russell to Hutt.
17. *Ibid.*
18. Acts of Council. W.A. — 6 Victoria, No. 5.
19. *Ibid.*
20. For a further description of these events see Essays on Immigration Policy and Population in Western Australia 1950-1901 by I.H. vanden Driesen. Essay I, pp. 14-48 and Essay III, pp. 62-95.
21. *Ibid.*
22. *Ibid.*
23. See Australia's Western Third by F.K. Crowley, pp. 32-58.
24. C.O., 18.159. 11th August, 1868. — Hampton to Buckingham (Encl).
25. The Statutes.
26. *Ibid.*, Clause 2.
27. *Ibid.*, Clause 1.
28. Master and Servant in Western Australia - 1851-1901 — F.K. Crowley. In Journal and Proceedings of the Western Australian Historical Society, Vol. IV, Part VI.
29. The Statutes of Western Australia — Ordinance 11 of 1873.
30. vanden Driesen, *op. cit.*, pp. 78 & 79.
31. *Ibid.*, pp. 62-90.
32. The Statutes of Western Australia — Ordinance 11 of 1882; C.O. 18. 1998. 21st October 1882. Robinson to Kimberley (Encl.).
33. Parliamentary Debates of Western Australia — August 14th, 1882. p. 136. Speech of the Attorney General.
34. *Ibid.*, August 15th, 1884 p. 189 — Speech of the Attorney-General.
35. *Ibid.*
36. *Ibid.*, pp. 190-96.
37. The West Australian. August 19th, 1884, p. 3. col. a.
38. The Statutes of Western Australia — Ordinance 20 of 1886; Parliamentary Debates of Western Australia — 1886, pp. 307-9; C.O. 18.207. 6th November 1886. Broome to Stanhope (Encl.).
39. Parliamentary Debates of Western Australia — 1886, p. 308. Speech of S. Parker.

40. The Statutes of Western Australia — Ordinance 25 of 1886.
41. Parliamentary Debates of Western Australia — August 30th, 1886, p. 556. Speech of Mr Wittenoom.
42. *Ibid.*, p. 558. Speech of Mr Randell.
43. *Ibid.*, p. 558. Motion of Mr Shenton.
44. *Ibid.*, p. 561. Speeches of Messrs Forrest, McRae and Layman.
45. *Ibid.*, p. 565.
46. *Ibid.*, p. 561. Speech of the Acting Colonial Secretary, Hon. M.S. Smith.
47. Parliamentary Debates of 29th January 1892, p. 396. Speech of the Hon. S. Burt, Attorney-General.
48. Parliamentary Debates of Western Australia — 26th February 1892. pp. 654-56.
49. The Statutes of Western Australia — Ordinance 28 of 1892.
50. Parliamentary Debates of Western Australia — 3rd February 1892, p. 449. Speech of the Attorney-General.

4

Mr. Justice Burnside: A Judge in Advance of His Times

Robert Bruce Burnside, Justice of the Supreme Court of Western Australia was first appointed President of the Arbitration Court in 1903. Several terms as President totalling almost ten years followed and during that period his most important contribution is generally believed to have been the establishment of the Apprenticeship system. However, a study of his rulings in the Arbitration Court makes it evident that Burnside's contribution went very much further. In his early years on the bench, and in particular between 1903 and 1910, he adopted approaches and principles which enhanced the credibility of the court in the public mind and gave it a reputation for benevolent fairness. Essentially a humanist, he had the courage to dispense justice with an equitable hand, at a time when the dividing lines of class were firmly entrenched, and to embrace interpretations of the law which were remarkably enlightened.

The first major issue on which Burnside left his mark derived from a decision made by his predecessor, Mr. Justice F.W. Moorhead, which had led to the establishment of a wage agreement known as the "Kalgoorlie Standard." In July 1902, mine managers in and around Kalgoorlie announced that from 1 August, the wages paid to certain categories of mine labour would be reduced. The Kalgoorlie and Boulder Miners' Union promptly took the matter to the Arbitration Court where it early became apparent that the ultimate intention of the mine managers was to go beyond the labour categories earlier mentioned and effect a general all-round decrease in wages. Wage rates varied in the different mines and the aim of the mining companies was to have the Court award as the minimum wage, the lowest rate paid for each class of mining labour in the locality. Management held that prevailing rates reflected the shortages of labour which had followed on the rapid development of the industry. However, labour supplies had now increased, and being in fact in surplus, justified the proposed reductions. The Union reacted by arguing for a schedule of wages which more than neutralised the suggested cuts, their claims being well in excess of the levels put forward by the managers. It was held that living costs on the fields had risen considerably and that in comparison wages had fallen behind. But to no avail. The award granted by the Court set wage-rates at levels which were unfavourable to the miners, being just marginally above the employers' suggested scales and well below those proposed by the Union.[1]

With this the "Kalgoorlie Standard" came into being. An early result was that in one mine after another employers cut wages to the levels set at Kalgoorlie and consequent Union objections brought a spate of cases before the Arbitration Court, where Justice Burnside had recently succeeded Moorhead on the bench.[2] From the outset, Burnside made it apparent that his sympathies lay with the miners. Observing that there was a "plethora" of evidence in their favour, he methodically set out to neutralise the effects of the Kalgoorlie judgment by raising the wages of all categories above the reduced levels imposed by the "standard." This was by no means a simple operation. Economic conditions varied markedly across the mining sector, towns serviced by the railway in particular enjoying lower all-round prices than those that were not. A flat general increase in remuneration would therefore have favoured some areas over others. Burnside decided that the solution lay in equalising real incomes over the mining area as a whole. Taking the Kalgoorlie scale as a basis he asked that unions in other towns should compare their conditions and cost of living with those prevalent in Kalgoorlie. Indicating that this would be "the only matter of importance requiring attention," Burnside called for evidence that would show "such a difference in the price of food, clothing and other things as would justify (an) increase."[3]

With this principle in hand, Burnside opposed all attempts by employers to bring wages down to the Kalgoorlie Standard. In one case after another he made allowances for location, climate and the resultant cost of living and set wages at levels well above the "standard" (though not nearly as high as those counter-claimed by the unions).[4] Out of these endeavours two slightly different schedules covering the various categories of labour in the mines emerged. One applied to the north Murchison district and the other to Leonora and its environs. The former was known to have higher living costs and in keeping with Burnside's prescription its wage schedule was 1 sh. per shift higher for every grade of labour than the other.[5]

These events mark Burnside's first major impact on the industrial relations scene. A second was soon to follow. Early in 1903, the judge extended the approach he had applied in the mines to an associated employment, *i.e.*, that of engine-drivers engaged by mine operators. In the north Coolgardie and Leonora districts mine-owners announced their intention of reducing the wages of all engine-drivers, irrespective of grade, to 13 sh. 4 d. per shift. This was such a sweeping reduction when the conditions prevailing in the districts concerned were considered, that the unions through their general secretary, communicated with the various mine managers, requesting a conference so that the wages question might be amicably settled. The managers refused to meet the unions and the matter consequently went to arbitration. General conditions in the two districts being different, the union put forward two somewhat different sets of wage claims, both well above the level announced by management.

Burnside again held in favour of the unions. Grades within the occupation were restored and conceding that there were differences in the cost to living between the two districts, wage schedules reflective of these differences were granted. Moreover, these not only reversed the cuts proposed by employers, but in all cases put wages well in advance of existing levels.[6]

The emphasis which Burnside placed upon the cost of living in employee-employer disputes inevitably led the latter to focus their arguments on the contention that there were times when the state of an industry did not permit the increase in wage rates required to compensate higher living costs. This argument was first put forward by a group of gold-mining companies in the Arbitration Court in October 1904, but it proved a stance which Burnside would not countenance, arguing that "the condition of the industry is not of so much importance as the cost of living. If the industry will not support a man what is the use of that industry?" One had in addition to be certain as to why the industry in question was depressed. "The moment this Court considers the state of the industry in regard to a proposed reduction in wages, I think, in justice, we ought to satisfy ourselves that the industry is reasonably well managed. If the management is bad, to reduce wages with the idea of relieving that industry would be like trying to fill a sieve with water."[7]

The judge's approach was no doubt laudable in times of general economic stability, but fraught with danger when economic conditions were adverse and employment was under threat. This was brought home to all concerned in a matter of months. In 1904 the gold yield began to decline; some mines were forced to cease operations and others to reduce costs as a price of their survival. Given the importance of gold-mining to the economy in general it was not long before the latter came to reflect the slump and employers began to examine more closely the areas where economies were passable. This brought to the fore the question of what constituted a minimum wage for various categories of work and was productive of frequent litigation and of subsequent disagreement between bench and employer.

Employers held that the minimum wage was the minimum payable to "the least skilled of competent workers"[8] — a definition which tended to bring wages down all-round. Burnside was aware of this, remarking that "... the employer always makes the minimum the maximum ... it becomes a standard wage."[9]

To prevent this occurring he declared the minimum wage to be "the minimum for the average competent worker;"[10] a step which led to a notable increase in payments all along the line. A significant result of the difference in approach was that even when hard times set in and Burnside acceded to an employer's proposals that wages be reduced, they were set at levels well above those suggested by management.

The latter first occurred in December 1904 when the Master Metal Workers called for a reduction in wages, since in their view, due to the economic downturn, wages in the industry were too high "... having been established when labour was scarce, work plentiful and the cost of living very dear."[11] The Metal Workers Labourers Union retaliated with a strong counterclaim and as no agreement could be reached between the parties the dispute ended in the Arbitration Court. Given Burnside's views on the estimation of the minimum wage, it is not surprising that his award set a wage schedule which for every category of workmen established a rate well above that proposed by the employers, though below that claimed by the Union.[12] Thereafter, this became a common practice in his Court and throughout the years of economic stringency (1904-1909) Burnside's approach to the cost of living combined with his assessment of the worth of the average worker, to keep wages at levels above those recommended by employers.[13]

In a move aimed at counteracting this policy by reducing the total wage bill through decreasing one of its components, it was then put to the Court that the application of awards should be limited to workers over the age of 21 years, and that a lesser payment should be prescribed for those who were younger. Burnside however, was not inclined to co-operate, pointing out that the Industrial Conciliation and Arbitration Act fixed the age of maturity at 16 and that everyone above that age was entitled to full pay, "I do not see how we can comply with the request to provide for the employment of boys at a lesser wage than the minimum, because any person at the age of sixteen years and upwards is entitled to demand full pay if you employ him."[14] There were dangers also that wherever possible a prejudice against the hiring of older persons would be established and this clearly was quite unacceptable.

As it became increasingly clear that Justice Burnside would not hand down rulings which favoured employer over worker; that he was objective in adjudication and courageous enough to set right what he perceived to be unjust, dealings in the court at times took on the appearance of a jousting contest between employers and judge. Whenever it seemed that an advantage could be won through challenging or re-interpreting some aspect of an existing agreement or by introducing new conditions, the attempt was speedily made by management. Burnside's tendency to hinge many of his decisions on the cost of living made the latter an obvious target and an attack on the concept came in the last quarter of 1904 in a dispute between 8 unions and 18 mining companies. The companies produced evidence in the Court to show that if the workers bought their goods in the cheapest market "for instance ... purchasing in Perth and then transporting them to their homes, instead of purchasing locally ... the cost would be considerably lessened." It was urged that the true cost of the article was the Perth retail price plus the cost of carriage to the purchaser's home, and not the inflated local prices charged in the various outlying townships.

The unions, supported by Burnside, were quick to challenge this reasoning. It was pointed out that cash would have to be sent to Perth with every order and this would present problems if the customers concerned were ill or out of work. It was unlikely purchases on credit would be agreed to, considering the distance between the Goldfields and Perth and the consequent difficulty in collecting debts. Moreover, it would take time to bring stores and other goods up on the railway (if one existed) or by pack-horse or camel, and the workforce had to live in the interim. Clearly the time was not ripe for such an innovation, which would have to wait until, as Burnside put it, "it could be inaugurated by some more powerful means than that of the individual miner." What this amounted to was that in the meantime, the status quo was preserved and no alteration in the court's method of calculating the cost of living was permitted.[15]

Acceptance of Burnside's interpretation of the cost of living did not rest unchallenged for long. In October 1907, another attempt was made to water it down, this time through an action brought by the Tailoring trade. Had it been successful, there can be little doubt that its principles would have been embraced by every other employment. The representative of the employers in the Arbitration court asked the court to adopt in extenso as the working schedule applicable to the trade, a scale which had been formulated in Victoria by the Wages Board in that state. It was commended to Burnside "as being as near perfection as anything which is the work of human hands can possibly hope to be!"[16] Despite the accolade the judge rejected the proposal outright, on the grounds that it was impossible "to adopt a Victorian Standard" in Western Australia. In his opinion, all the available evidence showed that the cost of living and the general expenses of life were well below those obtaining locally, hence it was impossible to cut wages to anything like the rates being paid in the eastern states.[17]

Burnside believed that the difference in the cost of living between Western Australia and Victoria at that time amounted to 15 per cent and throughout the first decade of the 20th century his awards tended to adhere to that differential. He was aware that this could occasionally put producers into difficulty, but he held that given the limited market in the West, many industries were over-supplied and competition was driving prices and profits down. This led him to observe that "that state of affairs ... can hardly be made a reason for reducing the wage of those persons who are employed in the industry." Here again we find an expression of Burnside's deep sympathy for labour, and couched in different language, his oft repeated refusal to accept the employers' argument that industry "could not bear higher wages."[18]

It must not be imagined that the judge was unfairly biased in labour's favour, coming down always on their side. An example of his scrupulous sense of fairness is nowhere more apparent than in his handling in June 1910 of a dispute between the Norseman Miners Union and the goldmining companies in and about that town. The employers called for a reduction of wages all-round, since the area had recently been connected by railway with the larger centres and many of the previously existing disabilities had been modified, if not actually removed. The union in reply argued for an increase in wages, on the grounds that railway extension was productive of more profit to the companies than to the workers as larger quantities of ore were being moved and the prosperity of the mines had greatly increased. However, Burnside's award reduced wages by around 2.7 per cent, a step which placed payments to the various categories of workmen about midway between the levels proposed by the employers and the union respectively. The reason given for this step demonstrates unmistakably the judge's impartiality and candour. As he put it, "I said formerly that where the absence of railway communication was made a reason for asking and for granting a higher rate of wage, when that absence no longer existed, when the railway was brought to that particular town, then the reason for the increase ceased and naturally the increase awarded ought to cease too."[19]

With so many disputes turning on the cost of living it became imperative that the concept be clearly defined. As shown earlier in this essay, definition was being achieved by instalments. The cost of living was made dependent on where one lived, on the climate and on whether railway connection with major centres existed. It was made independent of prices in Perth and of the level of living costs in Victoria, but never was a comprehensive definition of the cost of living and its relationship to a fair wage arrived at. Burnside, who was the presiding judge throughout, grew tired of this piecemeal process, and when dealing with a dispute in June 1910, between the Butchers' Employees Union and their employers, attempted a conclusive settlement of the issue.

Remarking that he did not wish to hear any more evidence on the cost of living, Burnside announced that he had arrived at a cost of living computation through keeping his own accounts, which he intended to use as the basis of his future calculations. Moreover, he declared his belief that even the poorest wage should go beyond the cost of living and provide the recipient with a decent livelihood. "I am talking about those things we eat and drink and which are good for us. I exclude intoxicants. The account I refer to included bread, meat, vegetables and tobacco for myself, because I think that can almost be considered a necessary these days. On this basis I have found that a man can live in this country for £3 a month. The cost of living however is only one factor in ascertaining what a minimum wage ought to be. For my part I do not desire to suggest that wages should be cut down to the bare cost of living. That would be ridiculous. In addition to the items mentioned, allowance would have to be made for rent, clothing, light, fire and other incidentals too numerous to mention. Then again, in ascertaining what the wage ought to be, I think that reasonable provision should be made for the uncertainties of life. I should like to see a system of insurance a little more common among what I call the working classes, but I very seldom hear any witness in this court state that he has to pay six pence a week towards life insurance. Apparently when he dies his dependents have to look after themselves. One must allow for incidentals in the way of sickness, while again I think every reasonable individual ought to look forward to something better than an old age pension, and he should also be able to save a little to enable him to occasionally enjoy a holiday of a day or two. All these things, I think, ought to be considered in ascertaining what is a fair wage but the cost of living is not the be-all and end-all. Too much importance has been attached to the cost of mere eatables and drinkables, which in my opinion do not form more than 50 per cent of the total cost. The incidentals which go to make up what I consider the necessaries of decent livelihood have been lost sight of altogether. If we have to deal with this matter in future, I hope the persons concerned will bear in mind that the scope of the inquiry might now be extended a little so as to include the additional items which should reasonably be considered."[20]

Burnside's observations on the living wage created considerable interest in the community and he received numerous requests from both public and press that his data be made public. The judge obliged with comprehensive details and a sheaf of tradesmen's accounts. The widespread of the items covered makes it apparent that Burnside did not set out to draw up a "working class" pattern of expenditure as distinct from patterns more suited to those higher on the socio-economic scale. He prescribed a diet of wholesome food, of the sort he consumed himself, and sought to set wages at levels which brought it within the reach of the lowest grade of labour.

The thrust of Burnside's comments and suggestions brings to mind the famous judgment handed down by Mr Justice Henry Higgins in the Harvester Case of 1907. As President of the Federal Court of Conciliation and Arbitration it fell upon Higgins to define what constituted a "fair and reasonable wage" and then interpret this in terms of money payments. Higgins decided that the wage could not be left to the forces of the market. If it was to be fair and reasonable he declared, it had to be sufficient to meet "the normal needs of the average employee, regarded as a human being living in a civilized community." In his view, the lower limit would be a basic wage set for the unskilled labourer and to this could be added such extra payments as befitted the special skills of the trained artisan.

In the drawing up of the basic wage the cost of living was an important input, though Burnside gave it much less weight than Higgins did. As noted above, the former considered the cost of living to be "only one factor" in computing a minimum wage and in addition to basic food, drink, clothing and light, went on to include tobacco, insurance and even savings sufficient to cover the cost of an occasional holiday. Higgins had fewer terms in his index, which covered rent, groceries, bread, meat, milk, fuel, vegetables and fruit. Clothing and light were not included and he specifically omitted tobacco, holidays and insurance. He clearly had a narrower conception of the "frugal comfort" he prescribed as a minimum.[21]

One cannot help but compare the rather diffident note which ran through Higgins' Harvester award with the confidence which characterised Burnside's judgment. This may well have been due to the latter's knowledge that he was not a pioneer breaking new ground, but was only taking further an approach which had been introduced in the eastern states some three years earlier. Moreover, he was surer of his data. His views were based on household accounts he had collected himself over a period of one month and could therefore trust; whereas Higgins had gathered information from housewives and tradesmen of whose veracity he was not personally certain.

Nonetheless, it is a fact of history that the Harvester decision is considered a landmark in Industrial Relations development, while Burnside's direction, despite its more comprehensive nature, has won scant recognition, even in Western Australia. No doubt this follows on one being a Justice of the Federal Court and the other a judge in what was then a relatively unimportant state. Yet, it is a high point in Burnside's career and makes evident his general humanity and sympathy for the working man.

The events of this time also brought to the fore the need to assess clearly the wage scales applicable to skilled and unskilled labour. The question had been dealt with before, with particular wage rates being assigned to specific employments which required prior periods of training, but with no clear, general demarcation between skilled and unskilled. At the federal level this general differentiation came with the Harvester case in 1907, when Higgins set 7 sh. as the minimum wage for unskilled labour. The rates for skilled workers were arrived at by taking a variety of awards already handed down and relating them to the new unskilled wage. The rates were set in proportion to the new wage, and the old ratios between categories were not disturbed. These were set by the employer — through market demand in modern parlance — and were accepted by Higgins on the grounds that "the ratio of wages paid by an employer is a tolerably safe guide as to the relative merits of the ... classes."[22]

In Western Australia the question was precipitated through Burnside's great interest in the development of apprenticeship. The Apprenticeship system fostered skill, which had to be recognised and rewarded in an appropriate manner. In July

1910 the wage for the unskilled was set at 8 sh. a day, Burnside observing that "... it is as little as a man can honestly keep himself, a wife and two children upon, in a position in life ... he is entitled to occupy."[23] Where the skilled man was concerned the judge fell back upon percentages. "I think he should be entitled to from 20 to 25 per cent more than the unskilled worker; he should start at about 10 sh. per day."[24] This payment clearly represented a monetary compensation for time expended in acquiring a training and embraced the concept of what is now called "opportunity cost." Burnside's approach was an advance on that adopted by Higgins, who as noted above, was disposed to leave wage differentials to the vagaries of market forces.

Given Burnside's tendency to look sympathetically on the demands of the worker and usually to grant wage increases — though not as a rule of the order asked for, an award handed down in August 1910 in a dispute between the bootmakers and their employers was of marked significance. In response to a claim for a minimum rate of 1 sh. 4½ d. per hour, a wage of 1 sh. 1½ d. was granted, *i.e.*, 12 sh. per week below the requested level. As important as the nature of the award, was the fact that it established the rate then current in the eastern states and so for the first time in Australian history placed the operatives in this industry in every state upon the same scale. In other words, the established view that a cost difference of 15 per cent existed between the west and the eastern states was now being denied.[25]

This about-face by the Bench led the Union representative on the Court, Mr William Somerville to lodge a strong objection. He admitted that there was in the court's records "a steadily increasing mass of uncontradicted testimony to the effect that the difference in the cost of living between here and the east is not what it was." But he believed that a margin still existed and that the award had implications for many other categories of workmen besides bootmakers since wages all-round could be forced down to levels prevalent in the eastern states. Somerville's objections were of no avail and the rates set down by the award became the legal wage.[26]

The seeming switch in direction by Burnside appears to have resulted from an appreciation of changes that were occurring around him. The gradual appearance of an "Australian" economy as the country was drawn together by improving communications and the development of the Federal administrative system, made it inevitable that production costs in the eastern states, amongst other things, should have a bearing on similar costs in the west. In other words, the protection of distance which had kept the western market separate had begun to disappear. As the competitive threat grew, steps had to be taken to preserve the viability of western production and Burnside's award should be viewed as a move in that direction. Clearer evidence of his intent followed a month later in an award regulating wages in the tanning and currying trade. With the exception of the unskilled labourers, who were awarded some slight increases on the wages previously paid them and which brought them up to the standard of 8 sh. per day, the minimum rates prevailing in the industry prior to the initiation of the dispute were those adopted by the court and prescribed in the award. This was done, declared Burnside, "to enable the industry to keep on in spite of the competition it suffered from the eastern states." The product from the eastern states was superior and it was only the lower prices in Western Australia that could keep the industry afloat. Burnside would have liked to have raised wages, but this would have pushed up prices, and led to the collapse of the trade and to a consequent loss of employment. The most he could do was hope aloud that wages in the eastern states would rise so that rates in the west could increase with it.[27]

With this decision, brought down in September 1910, we reach the close of a phase in Western Australian industrial relations history. By then a number of fundamentals which assured equity to those who sought the intervention of the State Arbitration Court had been established, largely through judgments and interpretations of the law by Justice Burnside. In the years immediately following, the drawing together of the Australian continent as an administrative consequence of federation and of widespread improvements in communications tended to give increasing prominence to decisions arrived at in the federal arbitration court. It became common practice for state courts to take many of the latter's decisions as a guide and in Western Australia Burnside followed suit, making increasing reference to federal practice. The principles he had earlier introduced however, remained undisturbed and stand as a monument to one remarkably ahead of his time.

Though Burnside's judgments in the Arbitration Court ceased to attract attention after 1910, he gained national attention in 1916 with a decision handed down in the Supreme Court and here again his views ran true to form. World War I was in progress and in 1916 a spate of strikes broke out, brought on by shortages, rising prices and long hours of work. With the threat of a general strike hanging over it the government decided to make an example of a small but active group of militants, the Industrial Workers of the World. Twelve of their number were tried in Sydney and convicted for conspiracy and sedition. In Perth, a group of 9 members were taken before Burnside, now on the bench in the Supreme Court. The accused were found guilty, but Burnside appears to have believed that their complaints were not without some merit. In marked contrast to the penalties imposed in Sydney, he prescribed suspended sentences, an act which led one of the accused, Montague Miller a well-known socialist, to applaud him from the dock, and to describe him as "a tolerant and gentlemanly judge."

Despite these several incidents in both the Arbitration and Supreme Courts, Burnside is virtually unnoticed in the Labour History of Western Australia. Contemporaries have had little to say about him and later-day historians have tended to downplay a contribution which is of notable significance.[28]

REFERENCES

1. Reports of Proceedings before The Boards of Conciliation and the Court of Arbitration, Western Australia (hereafter RPBCA) — Vol. 1, 1901-03, pp. 45-54; The West Australian (hereafter W.A.) 16-7-1902, p. 8; 22-7-1902, pp. 4 and 5; 23-8-1902, p. 7.

2. RPBCA – Vol. I, pp. 111-15; *Ibid.*, pp. 117-19; WA, 17-1-1903, p. 7; 20-1-1903, pp. 4 and 5; 3-2-1903, p. 6; 4-2-1903, p. 5; 3-3-1903, p. 2.
3. RPBCA – Vol. I, pp. 135-44.
4. RPBCA – Vol. I, pp. 145-48.
5. *Ibid.*
6. RPBCA – Vol. I, pp. 149-51; *Ibid.*, pp. 152-54.
7. RPBCA – Vol. III, p. 128.
8. RPBCA – Vol. III, p. 137.
9. RPBCA – Vol. III, p. 158.
10. *Ibid.*, pp. 136, 158-59.
11. RPBCA – Vol. III, p. 141.
12. RPBCA – Vol. III, pp. 136, 140 and 142.
13. RPBCA – Vols. III - VIII.
14. RPBCA – Vol. III, p. 171; W.A., 1-11-1904 p. 2.
15. RPBCA – Vol. III, p. 172-73.
16. RPBCA – Vol. IV, p. 103.
17. RPBCA – Vol. VI, p. 104.
18. RPBCA – Vol. IX, pp. 37-46; W.A., 12-4-1910, p. 3; 13-4-1910, p. 8; 15-4-1910, p. 8; 17-6-1910, p. 2.
19. RPBCA – Vol. IX, pp. 48-54; W.A., 21-4-1910, p. 5; 22-4-1910, pp. 5-6; 17-6-1910, p. 6.
20. RPBCA – Vol. IX, pp. 68, 77-78; W.A., 8-6-1910, p. 4.
21. The Sunshine Harvester Case, 1907, 2 Commonwealth Arbitration Reports, 2-32.
22. *Ibid.*
23. RPBCA – Vol. IX, p. 113.
24. *Ibid.*, p. 110.
25. RPBCA – Vol. IX, p. 148; W.A., 31-8-1910, p. 2.
26. *Ibid.*
27. RPBCA – Vol. IX, p. 178; W.A., 30-9-1910, p. 3.
28. *Australian Dictionary of Biography*, Vol. 7 – 1891-1939, pp. 491-92.

5

THE COMING OF EMPLOYERS' LIABILITY

The last decade of the 19th century was a period of concentrated and significant change in Western Australia, touching all fronts be they political, economic or social. In 1890, the colony had become a self-governing member of the British Empire, with a constitution closely resembling those already in place in the eastern Australian colonies. This improvement in political status enabled the government to embark on a large-scale borrowing programme and the first Premier of Western Australia, John Forrest (later Sir) initiated a number of important public works, which were in the main either directly or indirectly connected with the growth of gold mining.

From small beginnings in the 1880s the gold mining industry had grown rapidly. In 1890, production reached 20,000 ounces.[1] A quick escalation in the population was an immediate result, as gold-seekers and a variety of artisans poured into the colony, taking numbers from 53,177 in 1891 to 179,967 in 1900.[2] An early consequence was the appearance of a bi-cameral legislature consisting of a legislative council elected by property holders and a legislative assembly elected by males over 21 years of age. Simultaneously, employee organisations concerned with preserving equitable conditions in the workplace emerged and it soon became apparent that politicians who ignored their demands could put their own interests in jeopardy.

There were two areas in particular where problems arose and in each of these protective legislation was not long in appearing. Of these, one had to do with the mining industry *per se* and the other with frictions arising out of wage employment in general.

Disputes over the relative rights of alluvial miners and mining companies seeking reef gold, emerged in the mid-90s when the latter began to compete with individual fossickers. Two mining acts, the first in 1895 and an improved version in 1898 were enacted to settle the issue. Both pieces of legislation have had considerable scholarly attention and are not further treated here. Suffice it to say that despite initial disagreements between the two parties, natural events rather than the law dissipated the problem in the first years of the 20th century. Alluvial mining waned rapidly with the running out of surface gold and practitioners who stayed on in the industry tended to become employees of the reef mining companies.[3]

As the scale of mining and manufacturing grew in Western Australia, accidents sustained at work became increasingly common and brought to the forefront the second major problem of these times. The injured workers found they were still subject to the old common law that had existed in England up to 1880. The law held that a workman impliedly accepted and was willing to bear the risks attached to any employment he was engaged in; and that if he suffered an injury he had no claim against his employer under the law, even if that injury was due to negligence or ignorance on the part of an employer or his agent.[4]

In 1880, the law was altered in England. Thereafter, no worker was impliedly contracted to bear the risks of the work he was engaged in and in certain specified cases workmen were entitled to sue employers for injuries sustained in the course of their labour.[5] This bill was not immediately extended to cover Western Australia, probably because circumstances in the colony did not seem to require it, but by 1890, driven in particular by the gold discoveries, conditions were changing rapidly and the need for protective laws was canvassed by the newly set up Trades and Labour Council and by a number of candidates at the general election of 1894.[6]

When the newly-elected Parliament met, one of the first bills introduced was a measure designed "to extend and regulate the liability of employers to make compensation for personal injuries suffered by workmen in their service."[7] This was practically an adoption of the English Act of 1880 and with it the operation of the common law under which workers were not permitted to secure damages was wholly reversed. The change was accompanied by conditions intended to secure the employer from liability for which he could not be held responsible. The injury sustained by the employee had to be due to a defect in the works, machinery or plant, or to the negligence of the employer or of the person acting under his orders.[8]

When introducing the bill in Parliament, the Attorney-General, Mr. S. Burt (Ashburton), held that the Act showed that the government had the interests of the working-class in mind and was therefore "far more liberal than many people were prepared to give them credit for."[9] This claim was immediately challenged by both the trade unions and the press. The secretary of the Trades and Labour Council, Mr. G. Chitty Baker, protested that Burt was conveniently ignoring "the fact that over twelve months ago the Trades and Labour Council had forwarded a petition to the Premier signed by 1,550 bona fide workers praying for a bill to be introduced ... but no notice was taken of it, nor was it even acknowledged."[10] Chitty Baker was supported by 'The Western Mail,' a popular newspaper of the time which declared that the bill was "brought by the government into the House in response to a generally expressed wish voiced at the last elections."[11] But Burt would have none of this, contemptuously dismissing the views of both TLC and press with the remark that those who asked for employers liability "knew nothing of what they were talking about."[12]

In the Legislative Assembly and the local press the new bill came in for trenchant criticism. It was pointed out that the government had taken for a guide an English Act which was already 14 years old and was "discredited to a great extent in the country where it was passed." No sooner had it become law in England, than it was found that its priorities could be evaded by employees "contracting out," *i.e.*, signing agreements whereby they exempted employers from the liabilities imposed under the Act. Apparently, this course was quickly resorted to. Times were hard and in the competition for employment those who refused to sign the required agreement had very little chance of getting work.[13] As a counter an attempt was made in 1893 to introduce an amending bill which prohibited "contracting out", but this was strenuously opposed in the Commons and was finally carried by a majority of only eighteen, 236 members voting for and 218 against. When the bill went up to the House of Lords for ratification it was severely handled and was returned to the Commons with the contracting out clause eliminated. The government would not accept it in this form and the bill had not yet become law when the Western Australian legislation went before the local parliament in 1894 with the recommendation that it be adopted wholesale, as it had been in most other British overseas possessions.[14]

Since the Western Australian bill was a copy of the English Act of 1880, the weaknesses of the one were reflected in the other. The first issue seized upon in the Legislative Assembly was the workmen's right to legally contract out of the rights and privileges conferred by the Act. Strangely, the Attorney-General, who introduced the bill, did not think it contradictory that if the Legislature passed an Act to give a remedy to workmen, that same legislation should permit them to contract out of that remedy! However, there were others in the House who did, notably Mr Walter James, the Member for East Perth, who was quick to argue that the clause could prevent workers from being free agents, since the first thing future jobseekers could be asked to do was sign an agreement contracting themselves out of the rights and remedies the Legislature had provided.[15]

The Press was also quickly on to this shortcoming and urged the Attorney-General to bring the bill "up-to-date," pointing out that in New Zealand where a similar bill based on the English example had been enacted, the offending clauses had been suitably adjusted to prevent the dangers predicted by James.[16] The Trades and Labour Council was even more forthright and in a long letter to 'The West Australian' described the Act as an "antiquated arrangement" that contained a clause which made the whole thing a farce.[17]

Another clause in the bill to which James took strong exception was that which covered damages payable for injuries sustained at work. The sum recoverable under the new law was not in any case to exceed the average earnings during the three years preceding the injury, of a person employed in the same grade in the same employment. James remonstrated that this principle was neither fair nor just. If an apprentice earning 5 sh. a week lost both his legs and was incapacitated for life, he would get £39 by way of compensation, and not a penny more!

In the House of Commons Act an upper limit of £500 damages had been provided for, but as shown above, the bill had yet to be agreed to. It was James's hope that similar liberal compensation arrangements would be arrived at in Western Australia before the bill finally became law.[18]

Concerns were also expressed by James and some other members with what might be described as certain of the lesser shortcomings of the bill, notably that penalties were not specified for negligent foremen or persons in charge of work done. Others again complained that it seemed that it was the employee alone who was entitled to consideration and the employer not at all. It was thought though, that these defects could be put right when the House went into Committee on the bill.[19]

The Committee stage brought Premier Sir John Forrest (Bunbury) into the picture for the first time. Forrest accepted the general thrust of the legislation and strongly objected to James's attempts at improvement. The bill, he argued, reflected the law of England and despite efforts to alter it in the home Parliament, that had not been done. Forrest's loyalty to England was absolute, as was his belief that England's laws were beyond reproach. As he put it, "as long as ... we were as far advanced as the great old mother country ... we were far enough advanced."[20] James's plea that even at that moment an amending bill along the lines he suggested was being handled by the House of Commons, went unheeded. If anything it appeared to irritate Forrest who charged that in all his speeches James assumed the role of a "special pleader for one side," and that "the honourable member said nothing about the employer; all his sympathies were with the other side (Mr. James: The weaker side)."

The Premier called upon the members to join him in rejecting what he thought were essentially one-sided proposals. This they did to such good effect that only one innocuous amendment of the several put up by James, i.e., that government also, and not only private employers, should be covered by the Act, were rejected with large majorities.[21]

James's proposed amendments and suggested improvements made good sense, but the hostility with which they were met and the ease with which they were defeated reflects Forrest's influence in the House. For example, James pointed out that in the bill the definition of "workman" was inadequate. It was specifically taken to mean "a railway servant, a labourer in husbandry or a journeyman, artificer, handicraftsman, miner or otherwise engaged in manual labour." The effect of this description was that unless a person fell within one of the described occupations, he had to prove that he was "engaged in manual labour" when an accident occurred or he could not claim compensation. But there were occupations which did not fall within those specially mentioned and where it also could not be said that a person was engaged in manual labour, for example, a bus conductor or a tram-driver. James proposed that this difficulty could be overcome if the expression "workman" as used in the New Zealand Act were to be adopted. This further reference to New Zealand infuriated Forrest who declared that he was not prepared "to follow the honourable member for East Perth in his unqualified fairth in New Zealand legislation." It would "be safer to adhere to the English law" and he called on the members of the House to give him their support.[22]

This appeal fell upon receptive ears. Most in the Assembly were sympathetic to the employers and believed that the latter would not stand for stringent legislation. If the law was made more rigorous, they might, it was thought, cut back on employment and the new law would react upon the very class it was intended to serve. Not surprisingly, the amendment when put was promptly negatived.

Undeterred, James continued to put up one amendment after another, some of which were quite advanced for the time and the place. There was, for example, the proposal that the Act should inaugurate a system of compulsory insurance to cover a provision that employers should be liable for all injuries to their workmen, unless they arose from the latter's own negligence. The very idea appears to have rather scandalised Forrest, who saw it as an attempt to penalise even good employers and not as a simple device to cover all workshop mishaps however untoward. Once again, he called upon the members of the Assembly for support and the amendment when put was negatived without discussion.[23]

James next turned to the issue of compensation, returning to his earlier criticism of the principle embodied in the bill, *i.e.*, that compensation be limited to a maximum of a worker's earnings over three years. He stressed again that in the case of a young apprentice who might perhaps have lost the use of his limbs, the total payment would be a pitifully insufficient £20. He proposed that the compensation recoverable should be any sum up to £500 that the Judge thought fair and reasonable. The amendment was put and negatived, but the issue was picked up again immediately after by some members of the Chamber who clearly had second thoughts about the low level of compensation offered. Forrest however refused to yield, arguing that if employers were made liable for substantial compensation, no more apprentices would be taken on. In fact, one could reach the stage where "we should soon have no employers of labour at all." This very apparent lack of sympathy signalled the Premier's feelings and his influence was such that the matter was allowed to rest without further discussion.[24]

Moreover, it must be borne in mind that there were many members who had no time for the very concept of an Employer's Liability Act, and who gave Forrest the backing to negative any recommendation he did not agree with. One of the most hostile was the member for the Gasgoyne, Mr. R.F. Scholl, whose comments at the end of the debate summed up the views of many of James's opponents (and of Forrest's supporters). In Scholl's view, "the question of employers' liability was more of a parrot cry from a few people, instigated in the first place by a small body of people who called themselves by the high-sounding title of a Trades and Labour Council, or some such name. They had never yet been able to ascertain the number and importance of that body. They generally saw the same names in print as addressing the meetings of this Labour Council, but he had never been able to ascertain how many people attended these meetings."[25]

Since the proceedings of the House were printed in the newspapers, Scholl's speech was soon common knowledge and was not allowed to pass unchallenged by the unionists. In a letter the 'The West Australian,' Mr. Chitty Baker, Secretary of the Trades and Labour Council, pointed out that with just three exceptions every delegate to the Council directly represented a much larger number of people than did Mr. Scholl as representative for the Gasgoyne.[26]

Scholl's aggressive remarks served as a precursor to an even sharper exchange later in the debate when James rose again with a further amendment. He now moved that "contracting out" of the rights and benefits conferred by the Act he declared illegal. This was, he held, the most important section in the bill for "it was absurd to say that men were free agents and to talk about freedom of contract, because they knew that to a large extent this was all nonsense at present." On this occasion James was able to muster a degree of support, most importantly from the Premier himself. Despite his earlier negative stance, Forrest now admitted that if they passed a law for the protection of workmen, it would not "be right to leave such a loophole for evading the law as there would be if this clause were not inserted in the Bill.... If the law was to be of any benefit at all, a person should not be allowed to contract himself out of it to please his employer."[27]

With the exception of the member for Nannine, Mr. F. Illingworth, who spoke soon after James and offered his full support, four other members took the floor after the Premier and their reiteration of his arguments leaves one with the impression that they were merely trying to please Forrest. One notable exception though, was Scholl who voiced his disagreement even more strongly than before. To him the bill "was the work of agitators" brought over from the other colonies and he "did not want this democratic, or, he should say, this radical element coming amongst us to agitate the minds of people here."[28]

Given Forrest's about-face, Scholl's protestations had no effect. The Attorney-General, who initially saw nothing wrong in conceding the right to "contract out" now also changed his mind, rather lamely declaring that government had thought it would be better that provisions of the sort proposed, "should be introduced into the bill in the course of its passage through the House, and after the fullest discussion."[29]

With two key members of the Lower House prepared to lend their support, the disputed clause was accepted and the Employers Liability Act was passed by the Legislative Assembly without even the formality of a division. This was received with acclaim by the local press, one newspaper declaring that the Bill had been dealt with "in a spirit of fairness and with an evident desire to give to both sides their due."[30]

To be ratified the Bill had next to be accepted by the Upper House, the Legislative Council, where it was introduced by the Colonial Secretary, the Hon. S.H. Parker. The main outlines of the Bill having been described and eloquently praised, Parker called on the Council to expedite its acceptance.[31] However, the discussion in Council raised a question which had not been considered in the Assembly. The Honourable F.M. Stone, the Member for the North, proposed that the benefits and privileges of the new legislation should not apply to "Asian or African aliens," on the grounds that "they are only engaged where white men cannot be employed."[32] How this could be regarded as a valid reason for drawing the suggested distinction was not explained, but its blatantly racial slant is obvious.

This objection introduced a new variable into the debate, pushing members into quite sharply defined camps. The Colonial Secretary immediately indicated his opposition, arguing that to pass the amendment would be tantamount to saying that "it does not matter if the workman is a Chinaman, how much he is injured." This view was repeated by a number of councillors and most forcefully by the Honourable J.W. Hackett (South-West). "I cannot understand why the life and limbs of one man, although he may be of a different colour, are not as precious as those of another, or why he should not have similar privileges to the white man." In addition, Hackett went on to point out that if the object of the amendment was to discourage the employment of alien races, the very opposite could occur as employers would find it an advantage to hire workers on whose welfare they could not be legally called upon to spend.[33] Another member, the Honourable J.G.G. Foulkes (South-West) put up the argument that the moral standards of the Mother Country offered a further reason for rejecting the amendment and charged Stone with disgracing the Colony since it had always been England's boast that throughout the British dominions the law dealt equally with black and white. The argument was quickly dealt with by those in opposition who showed that in parts of the Empire and indeed, even in Western Australia, coloured and white were not treated the same. So strongly did this group favour Stone's views that they pressed Council for a division on the amendment. In the event, the latter was lost, though not by much, seven voting in favour and ten against.[34] The closeness of the vote however, is a good index to the depth of racial prejudice then current in Western Australia.

Assented to on 10th October 1894, the Act passed into the body of WA law as 58 Vict. No. 3 and remained unchanged for a period of 57 years. Its final removal from the Statute book came with the passage of the Law Reform (Common Employment) Act, No. 29 of 1951, whereafter an employee had the same rights and claims against his employer as a stranger would have and the Employers Liability Act* had no further application.[35]

REFERENCES

1. F.K. Crowley, *Australia's Western Third* (London, 1960), p. 86.
2. Western Australian, Year Book, 1902-4, p. 1152.
3. I.H. vanden Driesen, 'The Evolution of the Trade Union Movement in Western Australia' in C.T. Stannage (ed.), *A New History of Western Australia* (Nedlands, 1981), pp. 366-67.
4. Western Australia Parliamentary Debates (WAPD), 2nd August, 1894, p. 114.
5. *Ibid.*, pp. 114-15; The West Australian (WA) 4-8-1894, p. 4.
6. *W.A.*, 7-8-1894, p. 6, *W.A.*, 4-8-1894, p. 4.
7. *W.A.*, 4-8-1894, p. 4.
8. *Ibid.*
9. WAPD, 2nd August 1894, p. 114.
10. *W.A.*, 7th August 1894, p. 6.
11. *The Western Mail* (WM), 11-8-94, p. 11.
12. WAPD, 2nd August 1894, p. 114.
13. *Ibid.*, pp. 116-17.
14. *W.A.*, 4-8-1894, p. 4.
15. WAPD, 2nd August 1894, p. 116-17.
16. *The Daily News* (DN), 6-8-1894.
17. *W.A.*, 7-8-1894.
18. WAPD, 2nd August 1894, pp. 117-18.
19. *Ibid.*, pp. 118-22.
20. WAPD, 14th August 1894, p. 216.
21. *Ibid.*, p. 217.
22. *Ibid.*, p. 218.
23. *Ibid.*, p. 220.
24. *Ibid.*, pp. 221-22.
25. *Ibid.*, pp. 239-40.
26. *W.A.*, 18-8-1894, p. 3.
27. WAPD, 15th August 1894, pp. 240-41.
28. *Ibid.*, p. 241.
29. *Ibid.*, p. 242.
30. *The Western Mail*, 18-8-1894, p. 18.
31. WAPD, 5th September 1894, pp. 468-69.

(* for a copy of the Act, see Appendix I.)

32. *Ibid.*, 6th September 1894, p. 496.
33. *Ibid.*, 6th September 1894, pp. 496-97.
34. *Ibid.*, 6th September 1894, p. 497.
35. WAPD, 11 October 1951, pp. 1059-60.

APPENDICES

Appendix I

An Estimation of the Cost of Living. Results of an Experiment by Justice Burnside

As reported in *The West Australian* of 17-6-1910, p. 3.

CONDITIONS OF EXPERIMENT

"The difficulty of obtaining reliable information as to the cost of living induced me to resort to actual experiment. During the month just passed (May) we had no servants, so the opportunity of making a test presented itself — my household comprised three adults only. On Wednesdays, Thursdays and Saturdays we always sat down four adults to dinner; on Sundays always four adults to dinner (midday) and supper, and on one occasion six, and another occasion five to dinner; four always to supper. I have also included my luncheon in Perth."

"The experiment was carried out as fairly as possible — no change whatever was made in our method of living. I have not included malt or spirituous liquors. The result speaks for itself. I have tabulated the result, and the figures in red ink (marked with an asterisk below) are an estimate of what I think might fairly be added in respect of the items indicated."

Summary of Expenses

	£	s.	d.
Total household expenditure	8	3	8
Luncheon in Perth	1	4	9
* Rent at, say, 10 s. a week	2	2	0
* Fire at, say, 5 s.	1	1	3
* Light, at say, 5 s. a week	1	1	3
* Water at say, 2 s. 6 d. a week	0	11	3
TOTAL	14	3	11

	£	s.	d.
* Clothing, say, per month	1	0	0
* Sickness, say, per month	0	10	0
* Entertainments, etc.	1	0	0
TOTAL	2	10	0
Food, rent, etc. (as above)	14	3	11
GRAND TOTAL	16	13	11

Divide by three £5 11 s. 3-2-3 d., or, say, £6 per month each adult person.

"As I have included my luncheon account in Perth, I think a fair reduction should be made for extra meals. These amounted to at least 21 in the month. I, therefore, allow 10 s. 6 d. off in respect of them. Two dogs are fed as well, and you will notice dog biscuits are included at 2 s. 6 d."

Burnside's view that one could live in Perth on £3 per month obviously refers only to food and drink. On his figures total maintenance comes out at roughly £5.10 per adult.

Appendix II

The Employers' Liability Act of October 1894

WESTERN AUSTRALIA

ANNO QUINQUAGESIMO OCTAVO

VICTORIAE REGINAE

No. 3

An Act to extend and regulate the Liability of Employers to make Compensation for Personal Injuries suffered by Workmen in their Service.

[*Assented to* 10*th October,* 1894]

BE it enacted by the Queen's Most Excellent Majesty, by and with the advice and consent of the Legislative Council and Legislative Assembly of Western Australia, in this present Parliament assembled, and by the authority of the same, as follows:

1. This Act may be cited as 'The Employers' Liability Act, 1894.' Short title

2. For the purposes of this Act, unless the context otherwise requires: Interpretation Imp. Act, 43 & 44 Vic., c. 42, s. 8

The expression 'person who has the superintendence entrusted to him' means a person whose sole or principal duty is that of superintendence, and who is not ordinarily engaged in manual labour.

The expression 'employer' includes a body of persons corporate or unincorporate, and the Governor or any Minister acting for or on behalf of Her Majesty or Her Majesty's Government within the Colony.

The expression 'workman' means a railway servant, and any person (other than a domestic or menial servant) who, being a labourer, servant in husbandry, journeyman, artificer, handicraftsman, miner, or otherwise engaged in manual labour, whether under the age of twenty-one years or above that age, has entered into, or works under a contract with an employer, whether the contract be made before or after the passing of this Act, be express or implied, oral or in writing, and be a contract of service or a contract personally to execute any work or labour.

The expression, 'Judge who tries the action' includes 'the Magistrate' of a Local Court and the Justices exercising the powers of a Local Court.

Amendment of law

Imp. Act, 43 & 44 Vic., c. 42, s. 1

3. Where, after the commencement of this Act, personal injury is caused to a workman—

(1) By reason of any defect in the condition of the ways, works, machinery, or plant connected with or used in the business of the employer; or

(2) By reason of the negligence of any person in the service of the employer, who has any superintendence entrusted to him, whilst in the exercise of such superintendence; or

(3) By reason of the negligence of any person in the service of the employer to whose orders or directions the workman at the time of the injury was bound to conform, and did conform, where such injury resulted from his having so conformed; or

(4) By reason of the act or omission of any person in the service of the employer, done or made in obedience to the rules

or by-laws of the employer, or in obedience to particular instructions given by any person delegated with the authority of the employer in that behalf; or

(5) By reason of the negligence of any person in the service of the employer who has the charge or control of any signal points, locomotive engine, or train upon a railway;

the workman, or in case the injury results in death, the legal personal representatives of the workman and any persons entitled in case of death, shall have the same right of compensation and remedies against the employer as if the workman had not been a workman of, nor in the service of, the employer nor engaged in his work.

Exceptions to amendments of law

Imp. Act, 43 & 44 Vic., c. 42, s. 2

4. A workman shall not be entitled under this Act to any right of compensation or remedy against the employer in any of the following cases, that is to say:

(1) Under sub-section (1) of the last preceding section, unless the defect therein mentioned arose from or had not been discovered or remedied owing to the negligence of the employer, or of some person in the service of the employer and entrusted by him with the duty of seeing that the ways, works, machinery or plant were in proper condition.

(2) Under sub-section (4) of the last preceding section, unless the injury resulted from some impropriety or defect in the rules, by-laws, or instructions therein mentioned; provided that where a rule or by-law has been approved, or has been accepted as a proper rule or by-law by the Governor in Executive Council, or by any department of the Government

or officer under or by virtue of any Act of Parliament, it shall not be deemed for the purposes of this Act to be an improper or defective rule or by-law.

(3) In any case where the workman knew of the defect or negligence which caused his injury, and failed within a reasonable time to give or cause to be given information thereof to the employer, or some person superior to himself in the service of the employer, unless he was aware that the employer or such superior already knew of the said defect or negligence.

Representatives of deceased employer may be sued

5. An action under this Act shall lie and may be maintained against the legal personal representatives of a deceased employer.

Limits of sum recoverable as compensation

Imp. Act, 43 & 44 Vic., c. 42, s. 3

6. The amount of compensation recoverable under this Act shall not exceed such sum as may be found to be equivalent to the estimated earnings during the three years preceding the injury of a person in the same grade employed during those years in the like employment, and in the district in which the workman is employed at the time of the injury.

In determining compensation, payments or contributions by employer to or for benefit of workman to be considered

7. In determining in any case the amount of compensation payable by an employer, the Court shall take into consideration the value of any payment or contribution made by such employer to or for the injured person in respect of his injury, and also the value of any payment or contribution made by such employer to any insurance or compensation fund to the extent to which any person who would otherwise be entitled to compensation has received or is entitled to receive compensation out of such fund. In any action the fact of any payment or contribution having been made by the employer as aforesaid shall not, of

itself, be any admission of liability on the part of the employer.

8. Where compensation is awarded in case of the death of a workman for an injury sustained by him in the course of his employment, the amount recovered, after deducting the costs not recovered from the defendant, may, if the Judge who tries the action so directs, be divided between the wife, parents, and children of the deceased, in such shares as the Judge may determine. Judge may divide compensation

9. Where the personal injury to a workman who is illegitimate results in death, the same rights of compensation shall exist for the benefit of his mother, or of brothers and sisters by the same father and mother, as if he and such brothers and sisters were legitimate. Illegitimacy no bar to action

10. An action for the recovery, under this Act, of compensation for an injury shall not be maintainable unless notice in writing that injury has been sustained is given within six weeks, and the action is commenced within six months, from the occurrence of the accident causing the injury, or in case of death within twelve months from the time of death; Provided always, that the want of such notice shall be no bar to the maintenance of such action if the Judge who tries the action shall be of opinion that there was reasonable excuse for such want of notice, and that the employer has not been prejudiced thereby. Limit of time for recovery of compensation Imp. Act, 43 & 44 Vic., c. 42

11. There shall be deducted from any compensation awarded to any workman, or representatives of a workman, or persons claiming by, under, or through a workman, in respect of any cause of action arising under this Act, any penalty or part of a penalty which may have been paid in pursuance of any other Act of Parliament to such workman, representatives, or persons in respect of the same cause of action; and where an Money payable under penalty to be deducted from compensation under Act Imp. Act, 43 & 44 Vic., c. 42, s. 5

action has been brought under this Act by any workman, or the representatives of any workman, or any persons claiming by, under, or through such workman for compensation in respect of any cause of action arising under this Act, and payment has not previously been made of any penalty or part of a penalty under any other Act of Parliament in respect of the same cause of action, such workman, representatives, or person shall not be entitled thereafter to receive any penalty or part of a penalty under any other Act of Parliament in respect of the same cause of action.

Mode of serving notice of injury
Imp. Act, 43 & 44 Vic., c. 42, s. 7

12. (1) Notice in respect of an injury under this Act shall give the name and address of the person injured, and shall state in ordinary language the cause of the injury and the date at which it was sustained, and shall be served on the employer, or if there is more than one employer, upon one of such employers.

(2) The notice may be served by delivering the same to or at the residence or place of business of the person on whom it is to be served.

(3) The notice may also be served by post by a registered letter addressed to the person on whom it is to be served, at his last known place of residence or place of business; and if served by post shall be deemed to have been served at the time when a letter containing the same would be delivered in the ordinary course of post, and in proving the service of such notice it shall be sufficient to prove that the notice was properly addressed and registered.

(4) Where the employer is a body of persons corporate or unincorporate the notice shall be served by delivering the same at or by sending it by post in a registered letter addressed to the office, or if there be more than one office, anyone of the offices of such body.

(5) A notice under this section shall not be deemed invalid by reason of any defect or inaccuracy therein, unless the Judge who tries the action arising from the injury mentioned in the notice shall be of opinion that the defendant in the action is prejudiced in his defence by such defect or inaccuracy, and that the defect or inaccuracy was for the purpose of misleading.

13. (1) Every action for recovery of compensation under this Act brought in a Local Court, may, upon the application of either plaintiff or defendant, be removed into the Supreme Court, in like manner and upon the same conditions as an action commenced in a Local Court may by law be removed.

Actions under this Act brought in Local Courts may be removed as other actions

(2) Actions under this Act in a Local Court may be consolidated by order of the Magistrate, in like manner as a Judge may order consolidation of actions in the Supreme Court; and for the purpose of preventing multiplicity of such actions, rules and orders may be made, varied, and repealed from time to time, in the same manner as rules and orders for regulating the practice and procedure in other actions in the Local Court; and until such rules and orders are made, the rules and orders governing the practice and procedure of County Courts in England, in actions under 'The Employers' Liability Act, 1880,' shall be in force and govern the proceedings as far as the same may be applicable.

And may be consolidated

Imp. Act, 43 & 44 Vic., c. 42, s. 6

14. Every covenant, contract, or agreement hereafter made or entered into, whereby any workman or person binds himself or his personal representatives, either expressly or by implication, not to claim any benefit or enforce any right under this Act, shall be null and void.

Contracts to forego benefits of Act to be void

W.C.F. ROBINSON
Governor

